Local's Trave

John Cagle

Local's Travel Handbook: Jekyll Island

2016 Print Edition

***

John Cagle

Local's Travel Handbook
A Jekyll Island Travel Guide
Print Edition
Copyright 2016 Firewave Media LLC

TABLE OF CONTENTS

INTRODUCTION

The initial concept for writing this book sounded simple enough; write a travel guide about Jekyll Island from a local's perspective. "Shouldn't take more than a few weeks," I figured.

That was pretty wishful thinking.

Eighteen months and many revisions later, this travel guide is the result. I began writing this guide with the intent of giving readers a first-hand account of Jekyll Island, leaving no stone unturned and no topic disregarded, but I soon discovered that would have taken years, and if someone wanted to plunge through 1,400 pages of text they'd likely seek out a copy of *War and Peace* rather than this guide.

What I decided on was giving readers a glimpse into the little-known facets of Jekyll Island, like pointing out a hiking trail that can't be found on a map, or grabbing a bite to eat without breaking the bank. Are you a birder seeking out coastal fowl on your next trip? I've written a section dedicated to helping you cross more birds off your life list. Plan on wetting a hook during your stay? The section on fishing will help you find the right rod and reel, choose the right bait, get licensed, shop a charter (if desired) and put you in a position to catch more fish. This guide focuses on all the attractions, things to do, places to see and outdoor activities you would expect to find once you got to Jekyll Island, all with an extra dose of local insight to guide you through your trip to one of Georgia's natural treasures.

This venture was a passion project for me. My family used to take vacations to Jekyll Island when I was a kid growing up in the 80s, and even at 32 years old today, I can recall those memories with clarity and nostalgia. My dad reeled in his first shark right off Jekyll's east shore with a rod and reel I've still got out in the garage, and I can even remember playing putt-putt at Jekyll Island Mini Golf; a facility that has changed little (if any) over the last thirty years. The creation of this book cost me countless hours, immeasurable research, several sunburns, a pair of worn-out boots, a handful of tick bites, a multitude of mosquito bites, a few grey hairs and two big lessons in humility: that nothing worthwhile comes easy, and writing is hard.

It is my hope that you find value in this travel guide. If there's anything I've left out that you believe warrants attention, please let me know and I'll do my part to make it right.

- John Cagle

How to Use This Guide

The 2016 print edition was designed to provide as much utility to the reader as possible within the confines of these pages, while directing readers to external sources should they find themselves wanting to explore a particular topic even further. Sections where we've eliminated online resources available in the Kindle edition have been replaced with helpful illustrations, maps, and tools to provide readers with a thoroughly useful guide.

Major locations and attractions we've touched on in the guide include a business name and address. All listing information is current as of January 1st, 2016. We've also included business phone numbers, as well as websites and Facebook pages when deemed appropriate.

Below you'll find a quick example of a typical business entry:

Jekyll Island Club Hotel
371 Riverview Drive, Jekyll Island, GA 31527
(855) 219-7338
jekyllclub.com

Few structures represent the Gilded Age of Jekyll Island better than the Jekyll Island Club Hotel. Morgans, Rockefellers and Vanderbilts once strolled these very grounds . . .

Travel Guide Disclaimer

We've gone through great lengths to ensure the information in this guide is accurate, timely, and helpful. It poses quite a challenge, however, considering conditions change on the coast as frequently as the tides. What may be a thriving beachside restaurant one day could turn into a vacant property touting a for-sale sign the next. Firewave Media–the publisher of this guide–will work hard to make sure all of the information in this guide remains relevant through updated guides in the future, but weekly corrections are simply not feasible. Should you find any of the information in this guide inaccurate, incorrect, or otherwise problematic, please contact Firewave Media by emailing us at firewavemedia@gmail.com. If something is amiss regarding your guide, we'll do everything we can to make it right.

Important Notices for 2016

The new Beach Village is open for business

Jekyll Island Beach Village is up and running. Several businesses have subsequently relocated from various places around the island to their new home at Jekyll's contemporary central hub.

Jekyll Island Beach Village is easy to find. Take Ben Fortson Parkway eastward and drive until you come to a dead end at the roundabout connecting North and South Beachview Drive. Beach Village plaza will be directly in front of you.

Most of the businesses once located in the temporary Beachview Shops area off North Beachview Drive have already moved to the new Beach Village.

685 Seafood has closed

685 Seafood's unique location next to Jekyll Harbor made it a must-see for any seafaring traveler with a healthy appetite for both seafood and sunsets. Unfortunately, the restaurant closed its doors near the end of 2015. The property has struggled in years past to keep tenants, even with its picturesque setting on the Jekyll River.

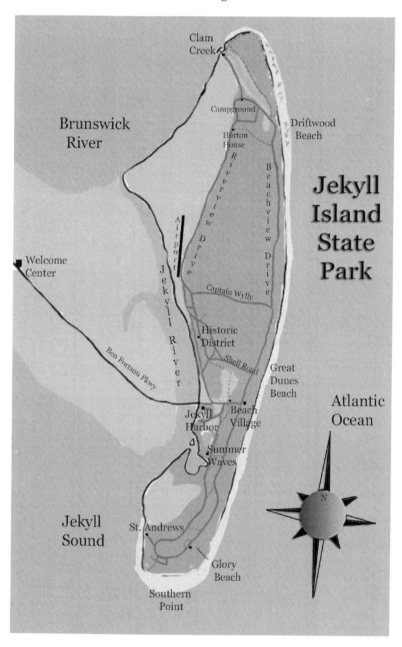

Clam
Creek

Brunswick
River

Campground

Driftwood
Beach

Horton
House

Jekyll
Island
State
Park

River

Airport

Riverview Drive

Beachview Drive

Welcome
Center

Jekyll River

Captain Wylly

Historic
District

Shell Road

Ben Fortson Pkwy

Great
Dunes
Beach

Atlantic
Ocean

Jekyll
Harbor

Beach
Village

Summer
Waves

N

Jekyll
Sound

St. Andrews

Glory
Beach

Southern
Point

JEKYLL ISLAND FACTS

Whether you've never been to Jekyll Island before in your life, or your next trip to the barrier island will be your 50th, there's plenty to learn about this unique destination off the Georgia coast.

Let's go over a quick list of facts to help you familiarize yourself with Georgia's Jewel.

Jekyll Island is one of four barrier islands located off the coast of Georgia commonly referred to as "The Golden Isles". These four islands include Jekyll Island, St. Simons Island, Little St. Simons Island and Sea Island. According to the Georgia Department of Natural Resources, there are a total of eight groups of islands off Georgia's shores, with Jekyll, St. Simons, Sea Island and Tybee remaining the only four accessible by car.

Jekyll Island is seven miles long from north to south, and a mile and a half wide at the island's center. The island has over 20 miles of paved biking trails, along with countless footpaths and inland wilderness routes to explore. Beaches line the eastern Atlantic seaboard, with the Intracoastal Waterway (called the Jekyll River locally) separating Jekyll's western shores from the mainland.

Many territorial claims have been made to Jekyll Island over the course of five centuries, including Spanish, French, and Native American, all before General James Oglethorpe put opposing assertions to rest by declaring Georgia an English colony in the name of King George II after landing in the New World in 1733. Oglethorpe was instrumental in the establishment of the new colony, which spanned from the Carolinas to Spanish-controlled lands in the south in what is now the state of Florida.

Several notable settlers called Jekyll Island their home during the 18th and 19th centuries, including Major William Horton, an officer in Oglethorpe's English regiment, and Christophe Poulain DuBignon, who left his home in France at the onset of the French Revolution to start a new life in Georgia.

The DuBignon family ruled over Jekyll Island from 1794 until 1886, when John Eugene DuBignon sold the family claim to the Jekyll Island Club Corporation. Rockefellers, Pulitzers, Morgans and Vanderbilts—to name but a few—would all come to call Jekyll Island their winter homes during the decades leading into the Great Depression and World War II. The extravagant cottages once housing the nation's wealthiest individuals make up the majority of the island's historic district to this day.

The Jekyll Island Authority–established in 1950–is responsible for the preservation of historical landmarks, island development and wildlife conservation on Jekyll Island. Development of the island is restricted to no more than 35 percent of high land per a 1971 law passed by the Georgia General Assembly, keeping the majority of the island in its natural, pristine condition and safe from over-development.

Over 500 residential homes are scattered across Jekyll Island, even though the entire island is owned by the state of Georgia. Homebuyers don't really own property on the island, but are actually purchasing long-term leases with the state.

Today Jekyll Island is known for its National Historic District, earning its place in the National Register of Historic Places in 1972, as well as its tranquil beaches, protected coastal wildlife habitats, and outdoor recreational activities providing visitors with plenty to learn about, see and explore.

* * * * *

PLANNING YOUR TRIP

If you've decided to take the Atlantic plunge and travel to Jekyll Island for your next excursion, then you need to consider a few things before heading this way. Some issues apply to everyone coming across the causeway, while others are only important for visitors staying in certain accommodations, so we've decided to start off with a little fee every person driving to Jekyll Island is going to get hit with: the toll fee.

Toll Bridge Fees for 2016

If you plan on driving across the causeway to the island, then you're going to pay a toll to get on the island, courtesy of the Causeway Toll Plaza. The tollbooths themselves look pretty classy, so at least you know your money is being put to good use. All fees are even amounts and include sales tax, so no need to scrape around in your cup holders for loose change.

Automobiles – Toll fees are $6 per day, $28 for the week, with annual passes running $45.

Oversized vehicles (over 8' tall) – $10 per day or $45 for the year. Weekly passes aren't available for oversized vehicles.

AVI Tag: One-time fee of $13. Must be purchased by annual pass holders. These annual decals expire after December 31st of each year so if it's already late in the year, consider waiting until January 1st to purchase an annual pass.

AVI Tags are also a great way to circumvent the long lines that tend to accumulate in the daily and weekly pass toll lanes, especially during the summer months.

Jekyll Island's Toll Plaza accepts a wide variety of credit cards including Visa, MasterCard, American Express and Discover. Cards actually process faster than cash, so consider using some of that plastic other businesses rarely accept when paying your toll fee.

No weekly pass is available for oversized vehicles; only daily and annual passes.

***

Islands Don't Have Everything!

It's funny how we get so used to the conveniences available back home that we just assume every destination on the planet has the same stores, restaurants, and accommodations.

"You mean they don't have a Wal-Mart?" is quite possibly one of the most common rhetorical questions locals hear from greenhorns making their way to Jekyll Island for the first time, so we'd like to take a moment to go over some things you should prepare for when coming to the island.

1.   Jekyll Island doesn't have a Wal-Mart. The closest Wal-Mart is about 9 miles away in the city of Brunswick at:

Walmart Neighborhood Market, 11 Glynn Plaza Brunswick, GA 31520. Phone: (912) 602-6145

2.   You're going without McDonalds, too. Hey, that's not always a bad thing, is it? If you still want to hit up that all-day breakfast menu, the closest McDonalds is about seven miles away at:

McDonald's, 1821 U.S. 17, Brunswick, GA 31520

3.   Jekyll Island doesn't do movies. With so much to do on Jekyll, why would you ever want to spend your trip in a theater? If you're still determined to catch the latest summer blockbuster, or looking to pass the time on a rainy island afternoon, then check out these two cinema locations nearby.

Island Cinemas, 44 Cinema Lane, Saint Simons Island, GA 31522. Phone: (912) 634-9100

Movies at Glynn, 100 Mall Boulevard, Brunswick, GA 31525. Phone: (912) 264-6058

***

Packing for Your Trip

Packing appropriately for your trip to Jekyll Island can mean the difference between a week of kicking back on the island with the sand between your toes, or endlessly traversing the mainland in search of the right brand of contact solution. As you may have already guessed, Brunswick is the closest city to the island, so making sure to check off and pack everything you may need before leaving the house will save you those time-consuming trips across the causeway.

***

Clothing

You probably have a good idea of how much underwear you'll need to last you through the week, but when packing for Jekyll, it's crucial to pack the right *type* of clothing–especially if you plan on camping.

The following should help you determine appropriate island attire based on the season you plan on visiting.

Spring – Early spring travelers should pack light garments for warmer daytime temps, while being prepared to cover up during potentially chilly nights.

Summer – Summer visitors will be greeted with afternoon temps that are typically in the 80s and 90s. Nighttime "lows" can remain in the mid-70s, so packing lightly isn't a problem.

Fall – The mercury usually doesn't dip below the daytime 70s until mid-October, after which jackets, long sleeves and light sweaters may be suitable.

Winter – Winters are mild and brief, with nighttime lows averaging in the 40s, and highs in the 60s from December through February. Still, it does get below freezing every once in a blue moon, so make sure you're prepared for potentially cold weather.

For a detailed analysis of Jekyll Island weather patterns that will help you pack for any time of year, visit Intellicast: The Authority in Expert Weather and enter the island zip code 31527.

***

Accessories

Sure, the hair products you're packing may contribute to fabulous flowing locks in the hot summer sun, but if you forget the one thing you should be putting on your head–like a big shady hat–your lobster face may end up getting more attention than a beautiful head of hair ever will.

Jekyll Island is located in a sub-tropical climate, and is much closer to the sun than most would ever realize. Many travelers know that sunscreen is crucial to wear in the Bahamas, but forget how important it is to wear sunscreen on the Georgia coast. That is, until they're lying in hotel rooms gingerly applying aloe to chargrilled skin. When you're packing for your trip, don't forget the following sun-wary necessities:

Hats – Big hats, small caps, it doesn't matter, just put something on your head. You'll get enough sun regardless of how often you wear a hat, so keep your face in the shade whenever it's possible.

Sunscreen – Sunscreen seems like a no-brainer, but many of us forget to pack this island necessity altogether. An $8 tube of SPF50 can set you back $15 to $20 on the island, so make sure you bring this one with you. Sunscreen is much cheaper on the mainland, so if you've forgotten yours back home and happen to be reading this on your way to Jekyll, just about anywhere you stop is going to be cheaper than waiting to buy it when you get here.

Sunglasses – If you don't already have a reliable pair of cheap sunglasses, then you'll definitely want to check out the shades on amazon.com long before heading to Jekyll. Breaking a brand new pair of sunglasses doesn't feel so bad when they only cost $5. If you're in the market for premium shades, on the other hand, consider stopping by Seaside Sunglasses, located in the new Beach Village. Just remember to watch where you sit.

Cigars – While we can't condone heavy smoking, nothing's wrong with enjoying a good stogie when you're on vacation. While there's not a bona fide cigar shop on Jekyll, you may find the sticks you're looking for at the Jekyll Island Beverage Center at Beach Village.

If you're seeking out a cigar specialist, and you don't mind taking an afternoon drive, then shoot on up to St. Simons Island, located north of Jekyll Island (14 miles when driving from island to island). There you'll find a little cigar shop that may have just the leaf you're looking for. Island Cigar Company, 1612 Frederica Road, Saint Simons Island, GA. Phone: (912) 634-0770

This location is approximately 18 miles from the center of Jekyll Island. Travel time is about 26 minutes one-way.

Chargers – Chargers have got to be the No. 1 forgotten device on every trip. Trust us, you don't want to have to resort to buying a cell phone charger on the island. Make sure to pack any device chargers you may need on your trip.

Umbrella – Jekyll's weather is typical of any coastal destination; sunny and clear one minute, torrential downpour the next. Don't forget to pack an umbrella, and if you're with your significant other and don't like getting wet yourself, remember to pack two.

Prescription medications – This is a big one, because the last thing you want to do is drive into Brunswick to get to the closest pharmacy. Over-the-counter meds like ibuprofen and Tylenol can be purchased across the island at places like Flash Foods and various locations at the new Beach Village, but scripts from your doctor require a long drive back across the causeway, so make sure you don't leave them at home.

Long sleeves – While it may be tempting to don only short sleeves and a bathing suit during your entire visit, odds are you'll want to venture off the beaches and inland at some point or another. If you're thinking about doing any hiking or biking through Jekyll's interior or marsh side, you may want to consider bringing long sleeve shirts and pants for the excursion. Long sleeves can also protect against UV exposure, just in case you're feeling a little "well-done" a few days into your trip.

Bug Spray – Jekyll is considered a semi-tropical location, meaning that its year-round climate tends to range from warm to hot in the summer, to mild and cool in the winter. Humidity is also an issue, with afternoon humidity levels rarely dipping below 60 percent. What does all this mean?

One word: *Bugs*. Coastal Georgia is known for its mild, pleasant climate, and with only a handful of days each year falling below freezing temperatures, the bugs around Jekyll are able to flourish year round.

Insects abound on Jekyll, but there are really only three main antagonists to watch out for: mosquitos, sand gnats, and ticks.

Mosquitos are known to carry West Nile Disease, while the ticks indigenous to coastal Georgia are known to spread Lyme Disease. As for sand gnats, well, they're just plain annoying, and can occasionally pack a nasty bite. Sand gnats are at their worst on so-called perfect days, when temperatures are hovering around 70 degrees. It's a good rule of thumb to recall the story of Goldilocks on this one: if it's really hot outside, the sand gnats won't venture out, and if it's chilly then they shouldn't be a problem, either. But if temperatures are *just* right, then be prepared to face a swarm of these pesky buggers, especially in late afternoon and evening hours around dusk.

Any one of these bugs may test your nerves on a trip, so bringing along plenty of bug spray is crucial to retaining one's sanity. When choosing a bug spray, there are several options to consider:

Bug Sprays with DEET: You've got three evil insect enemies that you may be confronting on your trip, and DEET products will effectively keep two of them—ticks and mosquitos—at bay. When shopping for a DEET-containing bug spray, make sure the spray you choose contains 20 percent to 30 percent DEET. Anything less won't be effective at keeping mosquitos and ticks far away, while research has shown that using more than 30 percent doesn't improve results. OFF! Brand's Deep Woods line contains 25 percent DEET, and is always in our backpacks when we head to Jekyll.

Avon Brand's Skin So Soft: The military swears by it, and locals love it. Avon's Skin So Soft, a product that was created for skincare, has been used in the war on bugs for years. Although many coastal dwellers will tell you that it's a great way to keep sand gnats at bay, most researchers agree that it does little to repel mosquitos and ticks.

ThermaCELL: Don't care for that slimy, greasy feeling many bug sprays and oils tend to leave you with? Then a ThermaCELL device may be just what you're looking for. ThermaCELL works by utilizing a portable butane fuel source to heat up a metal plate, in turn giving off allethrin vapors creating a protective cloud from a multitude of creepy crawlers and buzzing bugs. According to ThermaCELL's website, allethrin is a replica of a naturally occurring repellent that can be found in chrysanthemum flowers. ThermaCELL states their product effectively repels black flies, mosquitos, and no-see-ums, all without applying it to one's skin.

****

Beach Gear

Beach gear is a line item that can certainly add up if you wait to get to the island to purchase it. You already know to bring plenty of towels, but consider the following items that may just make your beach trip a little more enjoyable.

Beach Umbrella Anchor – Having plenty of umbrellas to cover you and the kids is one thing, but forgetting to bring an easy-to-install anchor for umbrellas to sit in? Well that can cause plenty of spectator amusement as you struggle for hours in the blazing hot sun to dig a suitable hole for your beach umbrellas, only to watch them get carried away by a burst of ocean air moments later.

Save yourself the trouble of digging your own hole by purchasing an umbrella anchor. You shouldn't pay more than $10-$15 for one, and they're available at several brick-and-mortar retailers like Target and Wal-Mart, or you can order one online at amazon.com.

Beach Cart – If you plan on walking from a parking area to the beach, you may want to think about picking up a beach cart. Beach carts are like all-terrain shopping carts for the great outdoors, allowing you to store your towels, coolers, accessories and beach chairs all on a single, portable cart. There are several models to choose from in the $70-$80 range on amazon.com. Being able to make it from the car to the beach in a single trip will make this portable accessory well worth it.

Beach Chairs – No, camping chairs don't count. If you truly want to enjoy your time in the sun, you need a chair that allows you to stretch out, relax, and take in those well-deserved rays. Cup holders are a nice touch, too. Beach chairs are another example of beach gear you'll want to buy on the mainland–or online–before you arrive on the island. Consider checking out www.amazon.com for the latest competitively priced beach chairs.

Sport-Brella – Got a newborn? Baby? Toddler? Then Sport-Brella has got you covered. Their selection of portable sun and weather shelters is perfect for quickly setting up a shady space to keep the little ones in during those long days on the beach. Most Sport-Brellas start around $50, with different styles varying in price from there. If you don't have kids then don't worry, these portable canopies make perfect beach nooks for grown-ups, too. For more information, visit www.sport-brella.com.

* * * * *

GETTING TO THE ISLAND

By Car

How does one get to Jekyll Island? There are several ways, with the most common route taken by automobile via Interstate 95–the primary interstate running north/south along the U.S. Atlantic coast. At a distance less than 12 miles from I-95, Jekyll Island is truly accessible to anyone with a driver's license and a reliable set of wheels.

From the north:

Take I-95 S to exit number 29 toward US-17 N/US-82 E. As you exit, you'll see a couple of signs leading the way toward Brunswick and Jekyll Island State Park, directing you to turn left up ahead.

Turn left at the stop sign onto GA-520 E. Be careful when crossing this divided highway; there isn't a (much-needed) traffic light at this intersection.

Follow GA-25 N/GA-520 E/US-17 N for 5.4 miles.

Turn right onto Jekyll Island Road/GA-520 E to stay on GA-520 E while heading toward the island. You can't miss the entrance on the right, and if you've crossed the Sydney Lanier Bridge into Brunswick then you've gone too far.

Stay eastbound on Jekyll Island Road/GA 520 E for another 6.6 miles. This will take you all the way into the island, across the Jekyll River and to the traffic circle that connects Ben Fortson Parkway with North Beachview Drive and South Beachview Drive.

From the south:

Take I-95 N to exit number 29, taking a right onto GA-25 N/GA-520 E/US-17N. Stay eastbound on GA-520 E (Jekyll Island Road) for 5.4 miles.

Turn right onto Jekyll Island Road/GA-520 E to stay on GA-520 E while heading toward the island. You can't miss the entrance on the right, and if you've crossed the Sydney Lanier Bridge into Brunswick then you've gone too far.

Stay eastbound on Jekyll Island Road/GA 520 E for another 6.6 miles. This will take you all the way into the island, across the Jekyll River and to the traffic circle that connects Ben Fortson Parkway with North Beachview Drive and South Beachview Drive.

***

By Air

Thinking about flying to Jekyll Island? You won't find any Delta or Southwest flights heading to this subtropical location, but there is an airport bearing the eponymous name of the island it caters to–the Jekyll Island Airport.

Jekyll Island Airport is a two-runway airport, with each asphalt landing strip occupying dimensions of 3,715 feet long by 75 feet wide. The airport operates without a control tower, is open to the public, and is a mere 11 feet above sea level.

Pilots arriving at Jekyll Island Airport should take caution on their approach, as deer are known to frequent the green grasses surrounding the two runways. The airport also saw an average of 74 aircraft per day for the 12-month period ending December 1st, 2014, according to AirNav.com.

For thorough FAA information on Jekyll Island Airport effective December 10th 2015, check out AirNav.com.
You can also visit the Jekyll Island Airport website at www.jekyllislandairport.com.

***

By Sea

Most of us have experienced the joys of driving or flying to our favorite destinations over the years, but how many people can say they've sailed to their favorite vacation spot? Sure, cruises are fun excursions, but nothing quite compares to docking a sailboat, runabout or yacht in the harbor of a charming southern island on the Atlantic coast.

If you're looking to take Jekyll by sea, then Jekyll Harbor Marina will be a necessary port of call.

Jekyll Harbor Marina is the island's premier marina for boats and yachts of all shapes and sizes. With a convenient location on Jekyll Sound, and just minutes from Brunswick and I-95, Jekyll Harbor Marina makes the perfect rest stop for boaters and sailors looking to dock their boats after a long day of exploring the Intracoastal Waterway.

The marina offers a dry boat storage facility that is fully enclosed, giving boat owners peace of mind when leaving their crafts in the hands of harbor professionals. If you're on a tighter budget, wet storage may suit your needs more efficiently.

Jekyll Harbor Marina has a variety of boating services, including ethanol-free gasoline and diesel, courtesy bikes and golf carts for boaters that are docking at the marina, and short-term guest dockage rates that include water, cable, and Wi-Fi access.

Noteworthy Discounts

When you're traveling by boat, every penny counts, so it's important to note that Jekyll Harbor Marina offers discounts for members of the following programs:

Boat US
Active Captain
Waterway Guide
Cruiser's Net

The current discounts include 10 percent off dockage for the aforementioned members at Jekyll Harbor Marina, and are subject to change at any time. Be sure to enquire about potential fuel discounts, too.

For more information on the Jekyll Harbor Marina, including checking up-to-date fuel and dockage rates, you can visit their website at www.jekyllharbor.com.

***

Around the island in thirty minutes

When it comes to transportation on Jekyll Island, you've got several options. The most obvious means of getting from point A to point B on the island is with your car—after all, you probably drove it here. Jekyll Island's two-lane asphalt perimeter is a little more than 14 miles in length, and can be cruised all the way around the island without making a single turn (once you begin on Riverview Drive heading north from Ben Fortson Parkway).

Why not kick off your vacation by taking a spin around the entire island? With an island-wide speed limit of 35 mph (unless otherwise posted), it shouldn't take you more than 30 minutes to explore the island's exterior on four wheels.

1.   As you're crossing the M.E. Thompson Bridge—the bridge passing over the Jekyll River before making landfall on the island—you'll be heading east toward the Atlantic. Once you cross over the bridge, you'll get in the first turning lane on your left.

2.   Make a left to cross the divided highway to get onto the Riverview Drive connector. Follow the connector 100 yards before turning right onto

Riverview Drive.

3.   After traveling on Riverview Drive for a half a mile, turn right onto Stable Drive. This will bypass the interior of the historic district, which can't be driven directly through to the north end. Don't worry, you'll have great views of the district to the west throughout the next stretch. You'll stay on Stable Road for one mile before it turns back into Riverview Drive.

4.   Traveling just over 3 miles from this point will place the main entrance to Jekyll Island Campground on your right. You can't miss the sign, as well as The Campground Country Store.

5.   Continue north from the campground on Riverview Drive. In a half a mile, Riverview Drive will become North Beachview Drive.

6.   The next 4.6 miles along North Beachview Drive showcase some spectacular scenery on the island's north end. You'll pass Driftwood Beach, along with the beach parking area, 0.7 miles from the campground entrance on your left. Most of the attention will be on your left toward the Atlantic as you pass several beachfront properties like Villas by the Sea, the Beachview Club Hotel, the new Holiday Inn, Great Dunes Park, and the Jekyll Island Convention Center. On your right, you'll pass Quality Inn & Suites, Jekyll Island Golf Club, Jekyll Island Miniature Golf, and Red Bug Motors Pizza & Pub.

7.   After passing the Jekyll Island Convention Center, you'll approach the roundabout at the new Beach Village shopping center, where GA-520 E/Ben Fortson Parkway intersects with both North Beachview Drive and South Beachview Drive. Throughout the course of this travel guide, this intersection will mark a central location for the purposes of this text, where the east/west portion of Ben Fortson Parkway splits Jekyll's north end from the south end.

8.   Drive through the roundabout and merge onto South Beachview Drive, where you'll continue southward along the Atlantic coast. Over the next 4.6 miles, you'll pass Days Inn & Suites, Hampton Inn & Suites, South Dunes Picnic Area, Jekyll Island Soccer Complex, as well as several parking areas and access points to nature trails, bike trails and beaches.

9.   After traveling 4.6 miles from the roundabout, you'll arrive at the entrance to the St. Andrews Picnic Area, on the southern tip of the island. Traveling straight will take you into St. Andrews, where picnic tables, restrooms, beach access and a wildlife-viewing tower await. Veering right officially places you on South Riverview Drive, and will take you back to your starting point.

10.   The next 2.4 miles along South Riverview Drive is a pleasant ride with little traffic along this stretch of two-lane, even during the busy seasons. The first half of this short piece will be marked by marsh views and creek beds, before passing Summer Waves Waterpark and Tidelands Nature Center on your left. A mere half a mile from the Tidelands Nature Center entrance will place Harbor Road on your left, where Jekyll Island Harbor Marina is located. Another tenth of a mile up from Harbor Road will put you right back at square one: GA-520 E/Ben Fortson Parkway. Turning left takes you back over the M.E. Thompson Bridge (and off the island) while turning right gets you to the roundabout at Beach Village.

Guess what? You've just driven around the entire island, and if you went the speed limit the whole way, it should've taken you about thirty minutes. Now that you have a better grasp of Jekyll's relatively small size, those bicycle rentals the kids and/or your significant other have been hounding you about shouldn't look so intimidating now.

* * * * *

HOTELS

If you don't have a relative or summer home on the island, don't worry; Jekyll has plenty of places you can stay. Eight hotels are scattered across the island, with lodgings available in the historic district as well as up and down the beaches from Driftwood to South Dunes.

Jekyll's hotels are without a doubt the largest commercial entities on the state-owned island, each with individual websites covering hotel basics like seasonal rates, bookings, and ever-changing events to a tee, so we're going to focus on information you won't find readily available on their home pages. With that being said, here are a few basics you should know before booking a trip through any one of these hotels on Jekyll Island.

Always book directly through the hotel

Once upon a time we called hotels directly to book rooms. Then, around the turn of the century and the dawn of the Digital Age, something strange happened: third-party companies started convincing us they could do it better.

Simply not true. When you book a hotel room through popular third-party websites featuring traveling gnomes, Captains of Obviousness, and sci-fi-television-stars-turned negotiators, you're basically dealing with a middle man when you really don't need one. Most major hotel chains–including those on Jekyll–are more than willing to price match rates from reputable competitors offering cheaper rooms on their own property.

Plus, when something goes wrong with your booking and you've completed it through a third party, it makes it difficult to go directly to the hotel once you're there and have them do anything about it. When you deal directly with the hotel, you know exactly who to go to if problems arise on your trip.

Understand what you're getting when you book a room

One of Jekyll's latest hotels is The Westin Jekyll Island, rising five stories above the east-coast dunes in the new Beach Village. This hotel opened its doors in 2015, so naturally you can expect a contemporary, fresh feel to the rooms and grounds. The Jekyll Island Club Hotel, by comparison, first opened its doors as a private clubhouse in 1888, and although it remains to this day a prestigious, well-kept property and excellent choice when booking a room, it's never going to replace its Victorian-inspired interior with something considered a little more "Feng shui" by today's standards.

The hotels on Jekyll Island make up an assorted collection of lodgings from wide-ranging eras, so it's important to bear that in mind when booking a room. If wicker furniture and retro lamps are items you find offensive, for example, you may do well to avoid certain suites available at Villas by the Sea. (Villas has over 140 rentals available, all with diverse interior design choices.)

On the other hand, if you'd rather be in the middle of it all, then booking a room at the new Westin will get you a stone's throw away from the newest shopping district on Jekyll. The Days Inn & Suites to the south will put you close to new retail, too, but places a little distance between your accommodation and the busy roundabout in front of the new Beach Village.

Whatever your hotel preference, just remember to do two things before you book: first, evaluate room photos online via the hotel website while comparing them to user photos on sites like tripadvisor.com; and second, make sure you call the hotel with any concerns you have prior to making a reservation.

Ask for discounts to island attractions and events

It's not uncommon for hotels to offer seasonal deals to local hotspots and businesses, and Jekyll's hotels are no different. Not only can you find great discounts on activities you were already planning for, but you may also discover a new special too good to pass up along the way.

Before you book with a specific hotel on Jekyll, make sure you check out the deals they offer to guests as a part of their specials and packages. Many hotels offer golf packages, romantic getaway packages, wedding and honeymoon packages, as well as deals on bike rentals, breakfast, massages . . . even free tickets to the Emerald Princess Casino Cruise Ship. Offers change all the time, so make sure to ask about the latest deals and discounts before booking your trip.

**

Jekyll Island Club Hotel
371 Riverview Drive, Jekyll Island, GA 31527
(855) 219-7338
jekyllclub.com

Few structures represent the Gilded Age of Jekyll Island better than the Jekyll Island Club Hotel. Morgans, Rockefellers and Vanderbilts once strolled these very grounds, escaping harsh winters during annual retreats reserved for the wealthiest of Americans. Since that time the club has opened its doors to the public, allowing anyone willing to book a trip the opportunity to peruse properties once exclusive to early 19th century aristocracy.

The Jekyll Island Club Hotel consists of more than just the original building, which opened to club members for the first time in 1888. There are currently five separate lodgings and one church comprising today's riverside resort, with a sixth property, the Jekyll Island Club Ocean Suites, scheduled for completion in the spring of 2017.

Staying at the Jekyll Island Club puts you at the heart of the historic district. If relishing the nostalgia evoked by the so-called Club Era is what you're after, then a stay at the Jekyll Club Hotel will leave your heart wanting for nothing. Guests can catch breakfast in the Grand Dining Room before heading out front to the great lawn to partake in an early morning round of croquet, or can opt to sleep-in before hitting the pool to catch some mid-afternoon rays while taking in a beautiful view of the Jekyll River from the comfort of a poolside lounger.

There is so much to discover in the Jekyll Island Historic District, and the Jekyll Island Club Hotel puts guests right in the middle of it. If Victorian architecture, fine dining and sophisticated service sound right up your alley, then consider booking your stay at the island's only 19th century clubhouse and resort.

Days Inn & Suites Oceanside Hotel

60 South Beachview Drive, Jekyll Island, Georgia 31527
(912) 635-9800
daysinnjekyll.com

Like the idea of being close to the Beach Village action, but don't want to be right in the middle of it? Then check out Days Inn & Suites Oceanside Hotel, located just a third of a mile south of the Beach Village roundabout on South Beachview Drive. This hotel is known for its premium location right on the Atlantic seaboard, along with oceanfront rooms at very affordable rates.

The property is older but well maintained, and the two new pools installed on the ocean side display their commitment to keeping up with consumer expectations. Many of the modern conveniences you would expect in a hotel are offered here, including free Wi-Fi Internet access, free continental breakfast, and free parking. There are also outdoor grilling areas, a hot tub for adults, a kiddie pool for the kids, the brand-new Snack Shack selling beer, wine, and of course, snacks, as well as on-site bike rentals making it easy to get your two-wheeling adventures kicked off from the comfort of your own hotel.

Room packages vary, with several rooms coming with full kitchenettes, others with only a mini-fridge, and some without both. Some rooms are also smoking rooms, with non-smoking rooms available, so make sure you specify which you prefer at the time of booking.

Days Inn & Suites is perfect for value seekers looking for a centrally located hotel that's right on the beach.

Hampton Inn & Suites Jekyll Island

200 South Beachview Drive, Jekyll Island, Georgia 31527
(912) 635-3733
jekyllislandhamptoninn.com

Hampton Inn & Suites on Jekyll Island is as cool as it gets. Nestled in the trees off South Beachview Drive, many of the rooms and grounds are shaded by the surrounding forest canopy, giving hotel guests a well-deserved break from the subtropical sun–if that's what you're looking for. If a little vitamin D is what you're after, you can head east to the beach via the Hampton's winding boardwalk through the woods and across the dunes.

Outdoor activities are available year-round at the Hampton, made possible by the seasonally heated outdoor pool and gas fire pit located on the beach side. What's better is if you're looking to head out early to get in a morning run or take in a sunrise breaking over the Atlantic, Hampton Inn offers to-go breakfast bags on weekdays for hungry Hamptonians in a hurry.

The Hampton Inn & Suites is also a dog-friendly hotel, so feel free to bring your four-legged friend on your next trip to Jekyll–just remember the hotel currently charges a $20 per night fee for canine guests. Located just north of South Dunes Beach and the southernmost hotel on the island, the Hampton is a great place to take your family, friends and/or Fido down to the beach for some well-deserved R&R.

———

The Beachview Club
721 North Beachview Drive, Jekyll Island, Georgia 31527
(912) 635-2256
beachviewclub.com

If 38 rooms nestled quietly under the shade of Spanish moss and windblown live oaks sounds like the tranquil retreat you're seeking during your visit to Jekyll Island, then consider booking a room at The Beachview Club. This charming boutique hotel is located on a quiet beachfront property north of the new Holiday Inn. The resort boasts immaculate grounds and attentively manicured landscaping, as well as a modest footprint, which naturally conveys a peaceful and relaxing stay.

Wi-Fi, flat screens, and all of the typical 21st century amenities are here. The Beachview Club also features a 16-person hot tub on the grounds, a heated pool, and convenient Adirondack chairs positioned at ocean side, making the perfect place to park your derriere with your beverage of choice and a good book.

The Beachview Club is currently undergoing renovations at the time of publication, with plans for completion estimated by mid-March 2016, but don't let that deter you from staying. The club has gone above and beyond to ensure every guest has an enjoyable stay during the renovation process.

And when renovations are complete, this resort by the sea is going to look like a million bucks. Every room is getting a complete overhaul, with new baths, fixtures, furniture, flooring, appliances, hot tubs . . . the works. The rooms that have been updated thus far evoke a very modern feel you'll appreciate the moment you step through the door. Make sure to visit their Facebook page to see just what's in store for the busy season of 2016. We're certainly looking forward to Beachview Club 2.0, and we think you'll like the new look, too.

———

Villas by the Sea Resort and Conference Center
1175 North Beachview Drive, Jekyll Island, Georgia 31527
(912)635-2521
villasbythesearesort.com

Some resorts have hotel rooms, others have villas. If the latter sounds like the resort for you, consider booking with Villas by the Sea Resort and Conference Center, located off North Beachview Drive on Jekyll's northern shores.

Villas by the Sea is unlike any other, with a diversification of uses to fit a wide variety of travel needs. Families and couples will find the serene location and spacious rooms perfect for relaxing vacations and romantic getaways, while organizations, businesses and enterprises can book events at their huge 9,000-square-foot conference center.

Have a really big family, big group, and big plans for your next visit to Jekyll? Villas by the Sea can handle it. The property is the largest resort on Jekyll Island, with 17 beautiful acres of scenic beachfront property waiting to be explored. Room options are immense, too, with guests having a choice between minis, one, two, or three-bedroom villas, ensuring you'll find the villa that's the perfect fit for you.

One important consideration you'll want to make is whether or not spending all day on the beach is important to you. That's because the beaches in front of Villas by the Sea are non-existent during high tide, where ocean waters actually reach the stairs that normally lead to the beach during low tide. The resort has done an excellent job, however, of compensating for their lack of a beach during high tides by constructing a 100-yard oceanfront deck complete with seating and a pavilion to accommodate guests seeking beautiful oceanfront views, as well as a huge swimming pool underneath a hardwood canopy centrally located on the grounds.

The resort is also a favorite among snowbirds, so whether you're looking to stay for a long weekend, or for months at a time, Villas by the Sea can handle all of your lodging needs.

———

The Westin Jekyll Island
110 Ocean Way, Jekyll Island, Georgia 31527

(912)635-4545
westinjekyllisland.com

Go big or go home. While it's not the Westin's official motto, perhaps it
should be. This five-story hotel rising high above the dunes at the new
Beach Village is the latest addition to Jekyll Island, and comes with all the
fixings one would expect from the popular hotel giant.

Opened for business in 2015, the Westin sheds new light on an island rich
in history, while breathing fresh air into the beachfront property located at
the end of Ben Fortson Parkway. The Westin has a stylish outdoor pool,
complete with a poolside lounge serving up your favorite cocktails, as well
as easy access to Jekyll's beaches. Other outdoor amenities include the
popular new Harry's at the Reserve, the Westin's open-air rooftop lounge.

While there's no way we could cover everything this incredible resort has to
offer its guests, we would like to point out some little-known services that
put the Westin at the top of the customer-service list. One such provision is
their New Balance Gear Lending Service. The Westin has partnered with
New Balance to provide guests with complementary running shoes and
workout apparel for the extent of their stay. It's simple: just call the front
desk, let them know your sizes, and they'll drop off everything you need to
get your fitness-center workout or beachfront run in. No more worrying
about packing your workout clothes, because the Westin has you covered.

Looking for an eco-friendly stay? Then consider taking part in the Westin's Make a Green Choice Program. Participation is easy: you'll receive a $5 voucher at participating food joints and beverage centers or 500 Starpoints for each night you decline housekeeping.

The Westin is also a dog-friendly hotel, so long as your dog isn't over 40 pounds. You can also expect a one-time $75 to bring Fido along, so keep that in mind when booking your stay. With high-rise rooms and high-end service, you'll be hard pressed to find another accommodation on Jekyll Island like this one. The views from the oceanfront balconies alone are worth taking in at least once in your lifetime. If you're seeking a vacation in the lap of luxury, consider booking with the Westin today.

———

Holiday Inn Resort Jekyll Island

701 North Beachview Drive, Jekyll Island, Georgia 31527
(912)635-2211
hijklresort.com

Another recent addition to Jekyll is the new Holiday Inn Resort, located on North Beachview Drive just north of Great Dunes Park. Everything you love about the popular Holiday Inn hotel chain on the mainland can be expected at their new Jekyll Island location, including 157 spacious rooms, clean accommodation, and a friendly staff ready to make your stay as pleasant as possible.

The Holiday Inn Resort has several family friendly amenities to keep little tykes occupied during your stay, including a beachfront playground and picnic area, swimming pool, as well as waterfront and beach activities for the whole family. While all activities vary by season, summer activities you can expect to find include scavenger hunts and hopscotch for the kids, along with family movie nights on an outdoor screen the whole family can enjoy.

The resort also offers in-house bike rentals, as well as beach chair and umbrella rentals for guests seeking a little comfort and shade down by the shore. It's important to keep in mind that while 10-20 feet of beach still exists in front of the Holiday Inn during high tide, the beach can be completely submerged when the weather is bad and coastal storms are moving through.

If you're seeking family friendly accommodations with plenty to keep the whole family busy at this brand-new facility, then consider making Holiday Inn Resort Jekyll Island your next stop.

———

Quality Inn & Suites
700 North Beachview Drive, Jekyll Island, Georgia 31527
(912)635-2202
choicehotels.com

Across the street from Holiday Inn Resort on North Beachview Drive lies the Quality Inn & Suites, the only hotel near Jekyll's Atlantic seaboard that isn't on the beach. Although the location on the west side of North Beachview Drive isn't oceanfront, it doesn't pretend to be something it's not, and as a result boasts the lowest room rates of any other hotel on the island (according to choicehotels.com, rooms start at $65 but, of course, are subject to change).

The location is great for families traveling on a budget. You may not be beachfront, but you're not far from it. A convenient crosswalk is located in front of the Quality Inn leading to the beaches, which are about 250 yards from the hotel's south end. By comparison, the beaches are about 140 yards from the main lobby of the Holiday Inn across the street, so walking an extra football field gets you an incredible discount on a room.

While Quality Inn and Suites is considered rather dated by some guests staying at the hotel, the service staff works hard to ensure everyone has a great stay. An important note to make is that according to hotel staff, this property will be receiving a complete overhaul beginning after the 2016 summer season, as is expected to be in premium shape by 2017.

If you're looking for a steal of a deal, and you're going to be spending more time outside exploring the island than inside your hotel room, consider saving some money by crashing at the Quality Inn & Suites.

* * * * *

DINING OUT

Dining choices abound across Jekyll Island, with eateries made to fit anyone's budget. Many of Jekyll's restaurants provide a plethora of menu options, as well as a charming dining ambiance suited for the southern coast. Should you opt for lunch in the historic district, you'll have horse-drawn carriages and 19th century architecture as your backdrop. If you prefer a larger dash of salt in your air, you can pick up a bite beachfront while letting the crashing waves of the Atlantic add to your dinnertime conversations in a setting you won't soon forget. Dinner options range from first-class meals at the Grand Dining Room, to a reasonably priced location known for breathtaking harbor sunsets called The Rah Bar.

Whether large or small, everyone is on a budget, and eating out on vacation tends to take up a large portion of vacation expenses. In an effort to avoid that sickening feeling that occasionally goes hand-in-hand with checking your bank statement once you get back home, we've arranged all of Jekyll Island's dining options in three price-based categories: on a budget, for a few pesos more, and fine dining. That way you can get a solid idea of what breakfast, lunch and dinner options fall in line with your spending plan.

We've also included a special section at the end, specifically for businesses specializing in sweets and desserts.

Island restaurants tend to come and go with the tide, so please bear that in mind when reviewing the dining choices listed below. All information, menu items and prices cited are valid as of January 1st, 2016 and are subject to change at any time.

***

On A Budget

Everyone likes to eat, but no one likes breaking the bank. You've already committed enough of your hard-earned cash toward island lodging, recreational activities and bug spray, so when it comes to grabbing a bite, why not save a buck or two?

Most families on vacation don't eat at 5-star restaurants for breakfast, lunch, and dinner. If you do, then you're probably getting advice from your personal concierge instead of reading this guide. If your anxiety kicks in and your appetite makes for the door as soon as you open up a fine-dining menu, then consider checking out these cost-effective eating joints on Jekyll Island.

***

Dairy Queen Chill and Grill
50 Ben Fortson Parkway, Jekyll Island, Georgia 31527
(912) 635-2573

Most people don't go on vacation with aspirations of fast-food dining in mind, but the Dairy Queen Chill and Grill will most likely be the first pit stop you see as you make your way across the bridge and down Ben Fortson Parkway, so we figured we would make this affordable meal option first on the list. After all, if you're coming off a long drive, you may want to pick up something that's affordable and fast rather than sitting down somewhere with the smell of the road still fresh on your shirt.

This particular DQ isn't your run-of-the-mill establishment, either. You'll find the menu items familiar, but the location is especially clean and welcoming, and the staff is very friendly, a character trait that comes with working on a subtropical island. You can run in and grab your food to go, sit down inside and catch some A/C, or eat under the shade trees at the picnic area adjacent to the restaurant.

Every red-blooded American knows the DQ menu like the back of their hand, but just in case you've been living in a cave since birth, here's what you've got to look forward to.

Price Range

The Dairy Queen Chill and Grill offers both breakfast and lunch/dinner menu items. Expect a limited breakfast menu with biscuits and gravy in the morning, followed by DQ classics like grilled bacon burgers, chicken wraps and chili cheese dogs for lunch. Several lunch combos run around $5, making DQ a great way to save a little cash while appeasing your fast-food cravings. (It's okay to indulge in a foot-long, fully loaded, chili-cheese-with-mustard-and-pickles slaw dog every now and then. Just remember to pace yourself.)

Hours of Operation

Sunday through Thursday, 7:00 a.m. to 9 p.m.
Friday and Saturday, 7:00 a.m. to 10 p.m.

———

Red Bug Motors Pizza

550 North Beachview Drive, Jekyll Island, Georgia 31527
(912) 635-9730
www.redbugmotorspizza.com

Craving a little marinara, a handful of pepperoni and a whole lot of cheese? Then consider stopping by the Bug to get your Italian on.

Red Bug Motors Pizza is officially Jekyll Island's go-to source for the best pizza on the island. Red Bug Motors Pizza is also wallet-friendly for families on a budget. Named for the red bug motors that can be seen touring Jekyll's main drags and side streets, Red Bug Motors Pizza is everything you would expect from a charming little pizza place.

Red Bug's brick-façade exterior could almost be mistaken for grandma's house, if not for the handful of Red-Bug cars parked out front. Red Bug Motors Pizza treats guests with their smaller, down-home setting that offers patrons both table seating or bar space indoors, as well as tables set up outside for those looking to catch a glimpse of the Atlantic while they eat.

Located off the main drag on Beachview Drive North and adjacent to Jekyll Island Miniature golf, Red Bug Motors Pizza and Pub is the perfect place to park your posterior after playing a pleasurable round of putt-putt. Absurd alliteration aside, the food's pretty good, too.

Price Range

Appetizers and salads run $5 to $10, pizza and pasta $8 to $18, with hoagies and wraps around $10. $3.50 gets you a hotdog and chips for guests on a budget. Soft drinks start at $2, with spirits $3.50 and up, bottled and on tap.

Hours of Operation

Monday through Saturday, 11 a.m. to 9 p.m.

McCormick's Grill
322 Captain Wylly Road, Jekyll Island, Georgia 31527

(912) 635-4103

McCormick's Grill, located at the Jekyll Island Golf Clubhouse on Captain Wylly Road, caters to golfers and walk-ins alike. The grill at McCormick's whips up daily what most would expect from a golf course restaurant, with a great selection of soups, salads, sandwiches and burgers. McCormick's Grill also has a breakfast menu, so if you forgot your morning coffee on the way to the golf course for an early bird tee-off, they've got the caffeinated cure for the morning drowsiness.

It's important to note that McCormick's only serves breakfast and lunch, and closes down for the day at 3:30 p.m. If you're looking for late lunch menu options on a budget, consider checking out some of the other restaurants covered in the "On A Budget" section of this guide.

Whether you're a walk-in from the beach who is looking for a bargain, or a golfer that's just wrapped up a round on the course, McCormick's Grill is certainly up to par.

Price Range

$2 cokes, breakfast items starting at $2, with sandwiches, wraps and melts running $4 to $9.

Hours of Operation
Breakfast is served daily from 7:30 a.m. to 10:30 a.m.
Lunch is served from 10:30 a.m. to 3:30 p.m.

———

Doc's Snack Shop
9 Pier Road, Jekyll Island, Georgia 31527
(912) 635-2820

Looking for a quick hunger fix while strolling through the historic district on Jekyll Island? Then head on over to Doc's Snack Shop, located next to the Morgan House, just a few hundred feet away from the main entrance to the Jekyll Island Club Hotel.

Cooking up the kind of food that hearkens to American favorites from a ballpark concession stand, this walk-up snack shop offers hot dogs, hamburgers, BLTs and BBQ. They also have a wide variety of popular beverages and snacks, which is good, because they're a snack shop.

Doc's is a walk-up restaurant, but they do have limited seating available on the wrap-around open porch. If you're looking for a quick lunch or just a few refreshments at an affordable price, check out Doc's Snack Shop.

Price Range

$3 to $10

Hours of Operation

Open daily 11 a.m. to 5 p.m.

———

Larry's Giant Subs

210 South Riverview Drive, Jekyll Island, Georgia, 31527
(912) 635-9283

Everything that you love about Larry's Giant Subs is available inside the Summer Waves Waterpark.

Larry's Giant Subs, known for their huge selection of made-to-order deli-style sandwiches, has an exclusive location inside the Summer Waves Waterpark on Jekyll Island. This real estate makes it convenient for waterpark enthusiasts and pool-goers to leave the coolers and lunchboxes at home while opting to eat lunch inside the park.

While the menu options are comparable to any of the Larry's Giant Subs food chains, the prices are a little bit higher, which is typical of restaurants located within waterparks. No worries, though, as Larry's Giant Subs remains a great value and convenient location for anyone spending a day at Summer Waves.

Price Range

$1.40 to $2 for fountain drinks, $5 to $7.50 for subs, $3 to $7 salads. Party platters feed 8-10 people and start at $40.

Hours of Operation

Daily 10 a.m. to 6 p.m., with extended hours during the busy summer season.

***

For A Few Pesos More

So 5-star dining is a little north of what you'd like to spend on a meal, but you're not sure whether your significant other will appreciate eating ball park franks and cold cuts while watching the sunset. To guarantee you don't remember Jekyll as the place you blew a perfectly good relationship once you leave the island, mull over this reasonable list of restaurants that Jekyll has to offer.

For the restaurants featured in this section, we're going to evoke the "Goldilocks Principle" once more: not overly expensive and not too economical, either, these subtropical establishments are *just* right.

***

Tortuga Jacks
201 North Beachview Drive, Jekyll Island, Georgia 31527
(912) 342-2600
www.tortugajacks.com

The only beachfront restaurant on Jekyll Island is sure to add a little spice to your life. Not only does Tortuga Jacks deliver on ocean-view vistas of the Atlantic Ocean, it is also Jekyll's only Baja Mexican restaurant, serving up favorites inspired by the best comidas y bebidas our friends to the south have to offer.

Tortuga Jacks is a huge property, so crowds and extensive waits in the lobby are rarely a concern. For those wishing to dine in, the restaurant has bar, booth and table seating, while exterior seating includes a 3,000-square-feet deck overlooking sand dunes, sea oats and island shores.

Even if you don't end up eating at Tortugas, at least take a moment to stop by the Baja Bar located on their beautiful new Atlantic overlook to grab a Jack's Margarita, kick back for a minute and take in the ocean view.

Price Range

Appetizers range from $6 to $12, salads start at $8, enchiladas and fajitas from $10 to $18, with Baja platters at $14 to $22. Kids have choice of cheese quesadillas or battered fish or chicken w/ sides for $5.

Hours of Operation

Open daily from 11 a.m. to close.

————

Driftwood Bistro

1175 Beachview Drive North, Jekyll Island, Georgia, 31527
(912) 635-3588 *(currently does not take reservations)*
www.driftwoodbistro.com

Coastal décor, southern charm and great value make this restaurant worth the visit. Driftwood Bistro, located inside the Villas by the Sea Resort and Conference Center on Jekyll's north end, offers Southern home-style cooking just like one would expect to find at grandma's house, with a few dishes that are exclusive to the coast.

If you're looking for something fried, you've come to the right place. Fried okra and mushrooms are favorites at the Bistro, with fried sampler baskets available for those having trouble deciding on what they'd like to try. A variety of greens like collards and green beans compliment entrees like catfish filets, meatloaf and tenderloin, sure to bring back memories of down-home cooking.

If you're looking for the favorite local dish then you should try the Wild Georgia Shrimp and Grits, the Bistro's most talked-about entrée. With reasonable prices for home-style cooking comparable to any inland dine-in restaurant, Driftwood Bistro is a must for anyone yearning for genuine Southern cuisine just like momma made it.

Price Range

Appetizers start at $5 and work their way up to $9.25 for a southern-fried sampler basket. Platters vary from $11.50 for a petite to $14.50 for a regular serving. $10 wraps, dips and sandwiches are also on the menu.

Hours of Operation

Monday through Saturday, 5 p.m. to 9 p.m.
Closed on Sunday.

———

Love Shack BBQ Shrimp and Yard Bird
11 Main Street, Jekyll Island, Georgia 31527 *(located inside Jekyll Market)*
(912) 635-2253

A little old place called The Love Shack is located inside the Jekyll Market. Catering to patrons seeking mouthwatering southern barbeque, wild Georgia shrimp, chicken wings, sweet potato fries and more, this small cafe serves up healthy portions of southern classics without depleting your food allowance.

If you're into fried oysters, make sure you order up a basket from The Love Shack–considered by many to be the best oysters on the island.

Price Range

Yard-bird baskets like chicken wings will set you back $9, whereas seafood baskets such as fried oysters run around $16. Baskets come with two southern sides: look for veggies like black-cyed peas, greens, coleslaw, sweet-potato fries, as well as the veggie of the day. Fountain drinks are in the $1-$2 range.

Hours of Operation

Open daily from 11 a.m. to 7 p.m.

———

The Rah Bar
370 Riverview Drive, Jekyll Island, GA 31527
(912) 635-3305
latitude31jekyllisland.com

Looking for a more affordable alternative to Latitude 31? Maybe an adult beverage or two? Then consider checking out The Rah Bar, located on the water in Jekyll's historic district. The Rah Bar–adjacent to its fine-dining counterpart Latitude 31–is a great place to grab a beer or margarita, pig out on some Dungeness crab legs, and take in the Intracoastal scenery from the Jekyll Island Historic Wharf.

The Rah Bar is everything you'd want in a casual, relaxed coastal atmosphere–no reservations required. Just walk right up, grab the nearest chair in the outdoor seating area, and a waiter or waitress will promptly offer you a wide variety of beverages while you enjoy the coastal breeze coming off Jekyll Sound. The Rah Bar also boasts live music for those wanting to engage their auditory senses, although nights vary–consider calling ahead for information on music and show times. (You can *usually* count on live music Friday and Saturday nights starting around 6 p.m.)

Whether you decide to partake in a low-country boil, peel-and-eat shrimp, or would rather just drink your dinner, The Rah Bar is THE place to take in a Jekyll sunset while feasting to your merriment in Jekyll's historic district.

Price Range

Winding down after a long day? Domestic beer starts at $4, wine by the glass at $7, cocktails at $10. Willing to get your fingers dirty? Peel-and-eat shrimp starts at $12, Dungeness crab legs at market price, with starters $5 to $12.

Hours of Operation

Daily from 11 a.m. until close

———

McGarvey's Wee Pub

20 Main Street, unit 100, Jekyll Island, Georgia 31527
(912) 574-2337
www.theweepub.com

Sports fans, beer lovers, and wee ones rejoice: Jekyll Island has a Wee Pub, and it's everything you'd expect from the hopping chain of coastal sports bars.

McGarvey's Wee Pub on Jekyll Island opened their doors in late 2015 at the new Beach Village, and so far the reception has been stellar. The fun-loving staff is serving up all your sports-bar favorites and much, much more. We're talking the Reubens, Phillys, wings, burgers and fries that are traditional game-day favorites, with specials like fettuccine Alfredo, fish & chips, rib-eye steaks, shepherd's pie, bangers & mash and Irish spaghetti wrapping up their list of inimitable entrées.

Naturally, the Wee Pub also has plenty of spirits on tap. Expect to find mainland favorites such as Guinness, Bud Light, Stella Artois, Shock Top, Smithwick's Irish Ale, Bass, Magners Irish Cider, Yuengling, Kölsch, and Michelob Ultra, as well as two local brews every serious beer connoisseur has to try: Cooter Brown Ale and Hop Dang Diggity IPA, both crafted by Jekyll Brewing. When it comes to spirits, Jekyll's only authentic Irish pub lives up to its reputation.

Don't let their unrivaled selection of suds fool you into thinking you can't bring the kids, either. Although Wee Pub hales as an island sports bar, the staff and atmosphere is very family oriented, welcoming guests to bring along the kiddos daily until 10 p.m. They even have a Wee Menu, made especially for youngsters and featuring items like hot dogs, grilled cheese, fried shrimp, chicken wings, spaghetti and more.

Price Range

The Wee Pub's lunch and dinner menu ranges from $6.99 on the low end, with their epic fried shrimp platter priced at a reasonable $17.99. The Wee Pub Weekday Special runs $7.99, and comes with your choice between three different sandwiches served with either a soup or salad.

The Wee Pub is proud of our military, offering 10-percent-off discounts daily, and a whopping 30 percent off for servicemen and servicewomen every Wednesday. They also offer 10-percent-off discounts for locals both long term and seasonal, as well as employees working on Jekyll Island.

Hours of Operation

McGarvey's Wee Pub is currently the only bar on Jekyll Island open every day until 2 a.m., and Sundays until midnight. The Wee Pub also has a special late-night menu served from 9 p.m. to 2 a.m. (midnight on Sundays), just in case you get hit with caloric cravings in the wee hours of the morning.

———

Club Café at the Jekyll Island Club Hotel
371 Riverview Drive, Jekyll Island, Georgia 31527
(912) 635-5203
www.jekyllclub.com

A second location is also open for business in 2016: Club Café at the Jekyll Island Beach Village. Call (912) 635-5188 for details and hours.

Looking to carb up and prepare for a long day of adventures on the island? Then consider stopping by Club Café at Jekyll Island Club Hotel, where you can find a wide assortment of pastries, muffins and sticky buns freshly prepared each morning for island explorers and beach bums alike. The Café also serves Starbucks Coffee along with popular breakfast items like fruit, pastries and cereal.

Club Café isn't limited to just breakfast, either, and offers a wide variety of sandwiches, salads, soups and wraps for lunchtime. They even provide picnic services and catering for those wishing to skip the interior dining and enjoy their meals in the Great Outdoors.

Price Range

Soups and salads range from $4 to $8 for chicken and tuna salad, deli sandwiches and wraps at $8 with sides around $2 each. Expect $2 to $3 for soft drinks, coffee and tea, with alcoholic beverages costing $4 to $7.

Hours of Operation

*Daily 7 a.m. to 10 p.m.

Hours vary for the new Beach Village location.

***

Fine Island Dining

You're on vacation, so why not splurge a little? Jekyll Island is home to the type of fine dining that puts coastal Georgia on the map. With three fine-dining locations nestled in the central historic district of the island, choosing a great restaurant for an incredible dining experience is as simple as taking a stroll along the past paths of the Rockefellers and Carnegies to your dinnertime destination. If you'd rather trade river views for sand dunes and seaboards, consider the fine-dining establishments located at the new Westin Jekyll Island.

Whether you're celebrating an anniversary, a birthday, or just an evening away from the kids, you'll have no trouble finding the best five-star service that Jekyll Island has to offer. So pull out that special dress or dinner jacket you've been saving for a luxurious night out and put it to good use by booking a reservation at one of these delectable dining locations.

***

Courtyard at Crane
375 Riverview Drive, Jekyll Island, GA 31527
(912) 635-5200
www.jekyllclub.com

Looking for fine dining in a casual al fresco atmosphere? Look no further. Courtyard at Crane is located at the historic Crane Cottage, near the Jekyll Island Club Hotel in the historic district of the island.

The rich history and tasteful architecture surrounding Crane Cottage could lead one to believe only dapper industrialists and oil tycoons donning three-piece suits would be welcome at this fine dining establishment, but Courtyard at Crane welcomes contemporary and casual patrons—just don't wear your swim trunks.

With a lunch menu ranging from reasonably priced soups, salads and sandwiches, to a dinner menu full of items such as maple and pecan-crusted salmon, veal strip loin and lobster Oscar, and a phenomenal 7-ounce center-cut filet mignon, Courtyard at Crane brings delivers nothing less than the best for lunch and dinner.

Price Range

Courtyard at Crane's lunch and dinner menus vary accordingly in price.

Lunch: Expect lunch entrees to run between $11 and $16, with $7 soups and salads ranging from $10 to $15.

Dinner: Entrees range from $21 to $36, with $7 soups, $10 to $15 salads, and $10 to $13 starters.

Dining Hours

Lunch: Sunday through Friday, 11 a.m. to 4 p.m., Saturday 11 a.m. to 2 p.m.

Dinner: Sunday through Thursday, 5:30 p.m. to 9 p.m.

Reservations for Courtyard at Crane are highly recommended. You can reserve your table by calling (912) 635-5200 or by visiting www.opentable.com.

———

Grand Dining Room
371 Riverview Drive, Jekyll Island, GA 31527
(912) 635-5155
www.jekyllclub.com

We hope you brought your dinner jacket, because the Grand Dining Room is an elegant experience that you won't want to miss. The site of some seriously fine southern dining, Grand Dining Room at the Jekyll Island Club Hotel presents guests with the most authentically southern gourmet dining experience the island has to offer. You'll take in the impeccable Victorian style, intricate white woodwork, and a welcoming trio of marble fireplaces that add to the Grand Dining Room's warm southern appeal.

Don't be surprised if you lose yourself in the romantic ambiance of the Grand Dining Room, especially during candlelight dinners that add a warm visual extravagance accompanied by the sounds of piano music softly filling the room. The Grand Dining Room caters to couples even more during the last Sunday of most months (call to enquire) where gourmet dinners are followed up by ballroom dancing.

The Grand Dining Room's ethereal setting is perfect for celebrating an anniversary, birthday, or any special event with the one you love. And because cellphone use isn't allowed in the Grand Dining Room, you can rest assured your magical southern evening won't be interrupted by an obnoxious ringtone. A formal dress code is required and is as follows:

For gentlemen: an appropriate dinner jacket is preferred. If you don't have one readily available, donning a collared shirt and slacks will still get you in the door. Try showing up in shorts, a t-shirt and/or open-toed shoes and you'll be politely turned away.

For ladies: Consider donning your favorite dress, skirt or even a pants suit, all of which are acceptable. They will also let you in with dressy sandals, as long as you're not wearing them with your classiest pair of Daisy Dukes. Shorts, t-shirts, swimsuits and/or cover ups aren't allowed.

Price Range

The Grand Dining Room at the Jekyll Island Hotel Club serves breakfast, lunch and dinner, with prices varying accordingly.

Breakfast: Club favorites featuring traditional breakfast plates range from $10 to $14, with starters like pancakes and waffles between $10 and $12. The Club Buffet offers a variety of breakfast choices and is currently $11.95. Available drinks like coffee, milk, juice and tea are around $3, with cocktails like Mimosas around $7.

Lunch: Expect to pay $11 to $14 for sandwiches, with specialties like the JP Morgan crab melt and Jekyll shrimp and grits ranging from $12 to $16. Soups, salads and starters are $6 to $14.

Dinner: Entrees like pan-roasted grouper, sautéed snapper, roasted vegetable en croute' and grilled stuffed veal chop are between $24 and $37. Starters, soups and salads are $7 to $16. At $8, the she-crab soup is something that everyone should try, even if you don't consider yourself a soup person.

Dining Hours

Breakfast: Monday through Saturday, 7 a.m. to 11 a.m., and Sunday from 7 a.m. to 10 a.m.

Sunday Brunch: Sundays from 10:45 a.m. to 2 p.m.

Lunch: Monday through Saturday, 11:30 a.m. to 2 p.m.

Dinner: Monday through Sunday, 6 p.m. to 10 p.m.

———

The Reserve

110 Ocean Way, Jekyll Island, Georgia 31527
(912) 635-4545
www.thereservejekyllisland.com

The Reserve is the premier restaurant at Westin Jekyll Island. Considered upscale yet casual, The Reserve delivers a contemporary dining experience in a relaxed island atmosphere, without sacrificing sophistication.

While some island restaurants tend to sleep in when it comes to operating hours, The Reserve is up with the sunrise, serving up three meals a day from first light to well after the sunset. Breakfast, lunch and dinner options fill the culinary needs of guests throughout the day, with the rooftop bar called Harry's at The Reserve filling in everything in between.

Expect traditional breakfast items such as pancakes, omelets, bacon and eggs, along with healthier choices like low-fat yogurt, fruit bowls and smoothies. The Lunch menu includes soups, salads, sandwiches and burgers, with dinner serving up only the finest entrees from land and sea, such as porterhouse lamb chops and center-cut swordfish.
Seating options provide guests with two contrasting experiences. Indoor seating is perfect for people seeking a modern yet refined dining atmosphere, while outdoor tables place guests in the heart of Beach Village, with incredible vistas of the Atlantic delivering an authenticate coastal dining experience.

Price Range

Breakfast beverages start at $3 and go up from there, with a bowl of market-fresh fruit setting you back $8. Larger portions like pancake platters and steak and eggs range from $13 to $20. The Lunch menu has soups and salads starting around $8, with main courses ranging from $9 for a grilled cheese to $29 for a salmon filet. The dinner menu has similar prices for warm-ups, with entrees like filet mignon, roasted chicken, cod, grouper, and shrimp resting in the $20 to $40 range.

Hours of Operation

The Reserve Full-Service Restaurant

Breakfast: 6:30 a.m. to 11 a.m.
Lunch: 11:30 a.m. to 3:00 p.m.
Dinner: 5 p.m. to 10 p.m.

Harry's at The Reserve: Bar and Rooftop Lounge

Open Friday and Saturday from 5 p.m. to 11 p.m.

———

Latitude 31 Seafood Restaurant
370 Riverview Drive, Jekyll Island, GA 31527
(912) 635-3305
latitude31jekyllisland.com

If you've already checked out the Historic District, then odds are you've seen the Jekyll Island Historic Wharf. If you haven't had a chance to visit the historic boardwalk leading to a fully functional marina overlooking Jekyll Creek, then why not take the time to make an evening out of it by dining at Latitude 31 Seafood Restaurant.

Latitude 31 is a short walk down Jekyll's historic wharf boardwalk, and caters to dinner crowds looking for an indoor dining experience. Not only does Latitude's menu fit its river-side setting with items like wild Georgia shrimp, crab cakes and jumbo scallops, but they also provide a little surf and turf for land dwellers seeking the best of both worlds.

Because of Jekyll's geographic location, there are only a few dining spots on the island where you can take in a truly magnificent sunset, and Latitude 31 is one of them. The sun sets due west of the wharf every evening until eternity, making Latitude 31 perfect for sunset and seafood connoisseurs alike.

Price Range

Latitude 31 Restaurant is a dinner establishment with seasonal hours. When in doubt, call ahead.

Dinner: Entrees are generally $19 to $36, with the exception of the lowest-priced menu item–sausage and meatballs over angel hair pasta coming in at $14. A few children's entrée items are $6 to $7. Soups, salads and starters are anywhere from $5 to $10, with deserts like key lime pie and the cheesecake of the day coming in around $6 to $7.

Hours of Operation

Dinner: Varies seasonally, but typically Tuesday through Sunday from 4 p.m. until close.

***

Sweets, Desserts and More

What list of restaurants would be complete without a few dessert dives to satisfy a post-meal sweet tooth? Everything that makes a dentist cringe can be found at one of these three island-sweets locations.

Jekyll Island Sweets Shop
150 Old Plantation Road, Jekyll Island, Georgia 31527
(912) 635-3135
Be sure to like them on Facebook.

If one shop in the historic district compliments a great lunch, it's the Jekyll Island Sweets Shop. The building the shop is located in was built in 1896, and was once the boiler house for Sans Souci, which can be seen to the west of the shop.

If Jekyll Island Sweets Shop were known for one thing, it would probably be for their fudge, although they've got a little bit of everything. Bear claws, chocolate macadamia, and peanut clusters are all common orders at the shop. Jekyll Sweets also keeps a variety of hand-dipped ice cream stocked, making the shop a popular stop on warm days. You can also pick up beverages here, too, in case you're looking for a place to grab some bottled water or a soft drink.

The historic building that Jekyll Island Sweets Shop is certainly dated, but don't let the location fool you. If you're in the mood for something to satisfy your sweet tooth, the treats here are timeless.

Hours of Operation

Open daily from 10:30 a.m. to 5 p.m. during the off-season, with longer hours kept during spring and summer months.

———

Fuse Frozen Yogurt
31 Main Street, Jekyll Island, Georgia 31527
(912) 319-2046
www.fusefrozenyogurt.com

Grab a cup and fill it up at the new Fuse Frozen Yogurt, located at Beach Village. Fuse has dozens of flavors of frozen yogurt, Italian gelato and sorbet to choose from, and at a mere 47 cents an ounce, this self-serve yogurt shop is more than affordable.

Expect to find your favorite originals like vanilla and chocolate flavors, along with unique additions such as blueberry pomegranate and toasted coconut. If you're looking for a taste of the South, go with "just peachy" or the coke float—two local favorites.

Hours of Operation

Sunday through Thursday from 11 a.m. to 9 p.m.
Friday and Saturday from 11 a.m. to 10 p.m.

———

A Sweet Shop Named Sprinkles
11 Main Street, Jekyll Island, Georgia 31527

Located at the Jekyll Market in the new Beach Village, A Sweet Shop Named Sprinkles sells cold treats, hot snacks, gourmet candies and more. Look for old-fashioned fudge, roasted peanuts, and a variety of other eats for you to take home. Don't forget to indulge in their homemade ice cream—by far their most popular dessert that has the whole island talking.

Hours of Operation

Sunday through Thursday from 8 a.m. to 8 p.m.
Friday and Saturday from 8 a.m. to 9 p.m.

* * * * *

John Cagle

SHOPPING ON JEKYLL ISLAND

Shopping in Jekyll Island's historic district is a unique experience conjuring images of late 19th century architecture, guesthouses, outbuildings, cottages, commissaries and infirmaries that have since been converted into gift shops, bookstores and art galleries. These quaint historic structures are filled with handcrafted jewelry, apparel, keepsakes and souvenirs exclusive to the island, with vendors lining the oyster-shell avenues offering a myriad of unique gifts you simply won't find in department stores.

Gift shops aren't exclusive to the historic district, either, and are scattered across Jekyll Island like the seashells lining the island's beaches. Perusing Jekyll's many gift shops is a treat for anyone who enjoys seeking out little known treasures and unique gifts to take back home. When you purchase a gift from one of Jekyll's shops, you're taking home a little piece of the island with you.

***

Jekyll Island Guest Information Center and Gift Shop
901 Downing Musgrove Causeway, Jekyll Island, GA 31527
(912) 635-3636

Located directly to the north of Jekyll's toll booths, the Jekyll Island Guest Information Center is a rest stop, gift shop, and island concierge all rolled into one. Here you can find out relevant island information about attractions, upcoming events, and sightseeing tours, along with insights into recent changes on the island. The friendly staff at the guest information center has a wealth of first-hand knowledge regarding Jekyll Island, so it's worth a stop.

The center also has a fully functional gift shop, complete with everything Jekyll Island you can think of: Jekyll Island t-shirts, Jekyll Island ball caps, stickers, key chains . . . you get the idea. The various island treasures offered for sale at the last store before leaving the island make this location a lifesaver for those looking to pick up last-minute gifts before heading back home.

There are also restrooms available with handicap accessibility, water fountains, and refreshments on the inside, with plenty of room to stretch your legs, including a short walk behind to building to the welcome center's bird-watching pavilion overlooking the marsh.

Hours of Operation

Monday through Saturday from 9 a.m. to 6 p.m.
Sundays from 10 a.m. to 5 p.m.

———

Beach Village Gift Shops

Jekyll Island Beach Village is the central hub for a variety of gift shops. Here you'll be able to find everything you need to tackle the beach, along with great gift ideas to take home. All of the shops listed below are located within Beach Village. You can see a map detailing shop locations at the end of this section.

Here's a brief rundown of the shops you can knock out in a single afternoon by taking a stroll down Jekyll Island's Main Street.

Whittle's Gift Shop
31 Main Street, Jekyll Island, Georgia 31527
(912) 635-2552
Check out Whittle's Facebook page by clicking here.

Anyone can buy a Plain-Jane hat and say they got it at the beach. If you're looking for a way to prove to your extended family you were thinking of them during your last beach trip, then consider stopping in Whittle's Gift

Shop in the new Beach Village. Whittle's touts the Jekyll Island logo on everything from t-shirts and hats to souvenirs and beach supplies, so they'll be no doubt as to where you picked up your significant others' apparel.

———

Brittney's Closet
10 Main Street, Jekyll Island, Georgia 31527
(912) 319-2083
brittneyscloset.com

If you have a stylish sister, classy cousin, graceful gal pal or fashionable frenemy named Brittney, then this store has pretty much everything you would expect to find in her closet. Sophisticated handbags, stylish shoes, jewelry, trendy tops, bottoms, and dresses designed to turn heads while befitting any fashionable female's refined tastes.

Hours of Operation

Monday through Thursday from 10 a.m. to 7 p.m.
Friday and Saturday from 10 a.m. to 8 p.m.
Sunday from 10 a.m. to 6 p.m.

———

Caroline's Gifts and Flowers
10 Main Street, Jekyll Island, Georgia 31527
(912) 319-2129
carolinesgifts.net

The name says it all. Caroline's Gifts specializes in unique coastal jewelry, accessories, and gifts, along with custom floral designs to fit any occasion. If you came to Jekyll to cruise the bike trails and have your beach cruiser in tow, be sure to check out their line of hand-woven bike baskets from Nantucket Bike Basket Company. They also sell handmade Jekyll Island mugs, wind chimes, stationary, books and more.

Hours of Operation

Monday through Saturday from 10 a.m. to 5 p.m.
Closed on Sunday

———

The Collection
21 Main Street, Jekyll Island, Georgia 31527
(912) 319-2056

Popular apparel includes Hook & Tackle, Southern Tide, Maui Jim, Panama Jack, and more.

Hours of Operation

Monday through Friday from 9 a.m. to 10 p.m.
Weekends from 9 a.m. to 11 a.m.

———

Life is Good
10 Main Street, Jekyll Island, Georgia 31527
(912) 635-4425
content.lifeisgood.com

Most of us have heard of the "Life is Good" brand, but if you haven't, well then it's time to familiarize yourself with their popular line of positivity tees, shorts, hats and more by visiting their new store at the Jekyll Island Beach Village.

Their brand is bent on spreading the power of optimism. They put their money where their mouth is, too, because Life is Good actually donates 10% of their net profits to kids in need through the Playmaker Initiative, which has supported over 5,000 social workers, teachers and counselors who are dedicating their lives to helping kids affected by early childhood trauma. Not a bad way to spend a buck, plus you'll get a t-shirt out of it.

Hours of Operation

Open every day from 10 a.m. to 7 p.m.

———

Seaside Sunglasses
31 Main Street, Jekyll Island, Georgia 31527
(912) 319-2024
www.seasidesunglasses.com

Like the name implies, this is the go-to shop for shades. Ray Ban, Costa, Coach, Gucci, Kate Spade, Vera Bradley, and Maui Jim are just a few of the big-name designer brands available. The storeowners have been in the eye-care business for over 10 years, ensuring you'll find nothing but the best eye and UV protection from a couple who have dedicated their lives to providing quality eye care.

Hours of Operation

Monday through Saturday from 10:30 a.m. to 5 p.m.
Sundays from 11 a.m. to 4 p.m.

———

Splash Resort Wear
10 Main Street, Jekyll Island, Georgia 31527
(912) 319-2096

Clothing and accessories made for beach and poolside living. Brands include Maui Jim, Costa, Southern Marsh, Panama Jack and more.

Hours of Operation

Monday through Friday from 9 a.m. to 10 p.m.
Weekends from 9 a.m. to 11 p.m.

———

Tonya's Treasures
21 Main Street, Jekyll Island, Georgia 31527
(912) 319-2068
www.tonyastreasures.com

This southern boutique store has a wide variety of women's clothing and accessories. Ladies swimwear, shoes, scout bags, seersucker, jewelry, hats, purses and home décor make up a variety of treasures just waiting to be found inside.

Hours of Operation

Monday through Friday from 10 a.m. to 6 p.m.
Saturdays from 10 a.m. to 8 p.m.
Closed Sundays

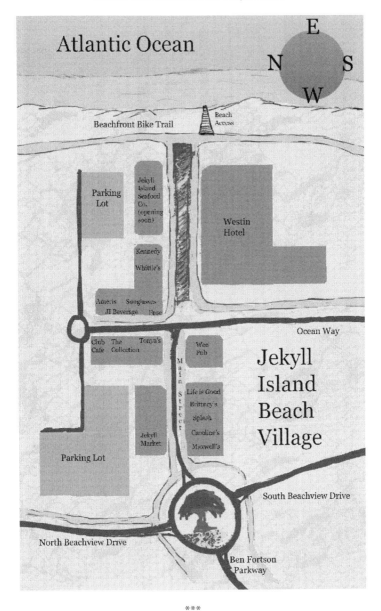

***

Historic District Gift Shops

Above The Dunes

21 Pier Road, Jekyll Island, Georgia 31527
(912) 635-3997
www.abovethedunes.com

Self-branded as an "eclectic, eco-friendly gift shop," Above The Dunes is a charming little store that will appeal to those seeking gifts considered to be off the beaten path. Here you can find art from local artists, handcrafted jewelry, old-fashioned and contemporary toys for kids, kites, handbags and more.

Many of the products for sale at Above The Dunes are made from recycled and environmentally friendly material. They are constantly updating their merchandise, so every visit is sure to be a unique one.

Hours of Operation

Open daily from 10 a.m. to 5 p.m.

———

Jekyll Island Club Hotel Gift Shop

371 Riverview Drive, Jekyll Island, Georgia 31527

Club Collections Gift Shop and Club Signature Shop
(912) 635-2600
www.jekyllclub.com

The Jekyll Island brand is ubiquitous throughout the Jekyll Island Club Hotel Gift Shop. China and glassware, clothing, golf accessories, books, specialty items and more all carry the Jekyll Island name in various forms and fashions.

If you're looking for a gift that's inherently Jekyll, then this is the place to stop. For the golfer in your family, plenty of hats, visors, umbrellas, golf towels, golf balls and other Jekyll Island golf gear is available both in-store and online. Local art enthusiasts: don't forget to check out their watercolor prints of various cottages and buildings located in the historic district.

Hours of Operation

Monday through Saturday from 8 a.m. to 5 p.m.
Sundays from 9 a.m. to 3 p.m.

––––––––

The Cottage
32 Pier Road, Jekyll Island, Georgia 31527
(912) 635-2643

Featuring a wide range of handcrafted gifts, The Cottage is proud to offer a variety of gifts made right here in the USA. All of their items are handpicked to fit their shop's distinctive, whimsical style.

Products include creative pottery works, wind bells and chimes, handmade candles, glass decorations and much, much more. Parents will also find a wide selection of toys that hearken to an age before electronic distractions, such as Folkmanis puppets, shark teeth, children's books, a pick-your-own-rock mix, as well as kid's apparel.

Hours of Operation

Open daily from 10 a.m. to 5 p.m.

––––––––

Georgia Sea Turtle Center Gift Shop
214 Stable Road, Jekyll Island, Georgia 31527
(912) 635-4444
www.gstc.jekyllisland.com

If your love for everything aquatic is unmatched, then you have to stop by the Georgia Sea Turtle Center Gift Shop. Located just inside the main entrance of the Georgia Sea Turtle Center, the shop has a variety of marine-themed shirts, hats and other apparel, as well as educational books, prints, and more.

The museum gift shop also has plenty for the kids, including children's books, games, and a plethora of stuffed animals: sea turtles, dolphins, manatees, and more. Gift-shop sales also help fund the center, which provides rehabilitation and educational services benefiting the fragile sea turtle population of the Golden Isles.

Hours of Operation

Open daily from 9 a.m. to 5 p.m. except on Thanksgiving Day, which is 10 a.m. to 2 p.m.

————

Goodyear Shop
251 Riverview Drive, Jekyll Island, Georgia 31527
(912) 635-3920
www.jekyllartsassociation.org

The Goodyear Shop, located within the historic Goodyear Cottage on Riverview Drive, houses artwork provided by members of the Jekyll Island Arts Association (JIAA). Because the art is displayed on consignment, the gallery is constantly changing, with new pieces coming in from talented artists and craftsmen alike.

These pieces are the real deal; you won't find reprints here. The Goodyear Shop maintains strict standards that every piece has to meet before being submitted into the gallery–only original paintings and photographs are allowed on the wall. Other prerequisites include membership in the JIAA, verifiably handcrafted and undamaged pieces, as well as meeting the needs and vision of the shop by being seasonally relevant at the time of submission.

Goodyear shop is only open four hours each day during the week, and six hours a day on weekends, so if you have an appreciation for meticulously crafted local art in its finest form then make sure to set a reminder in your phone so you don't miss out on the must-see Goodyear gallery.

Hours of Operation

Monday through Friday from 12 p.m. to 4 p.m.

Weekends from 10 a.m. to 4 p.m.

———

Gypsea Glass
13 Pier Road, Jekyll Island, Georgia 31527
(912) 635-9797
www.gypseaglass.com

Gypsea Glass isn't just a place where you can buy hand-blown or lamp-work glass. Here you can actually see glass sculptors meticulously create intricate pieces of glasswork one at a time right before your very eyes. No two sculptures are alike, meaning every piece available for sale within the shop is the only one of its kind.

Not only do the glass-blowing experts of Gypsea Glass create their own glassworks to stock the shelves, they also display the work of other local glass artists in their shop. These pieces range from stained glass ornaments, pendants and sculptures, to glass jewels and marine-themed adornments. You don't want to miss one of their demonstrations, so stop by if you're in the area or give them a call ahead of your visit to see when the next glass-sculpting session is.

Hours of Operation

Open daily from 10 a.m. to 5 p.m.

————

The Island House
17 Pier Road, Jekyll Island, Georgia 31527
(912) 635-2632

The Island House is a small retail shop located in the historic district of Jekyll Island. Call with inquiries.

Hours of Operation

Open daily from 10 a.m. to 5:30 p.m.

————

Jekyll Island Museum Gift Shop
100 Stable Road, Jekyll Island, Georgia 31527
(912) 635-4168
www.jekyllisland.com

The Jekyll Island Museum Gift Shop is located in the old horse stables just off the eponymously named Stable Road. Club-member horse stalls that once housed esteemed steeds belonging Rockefellers, Pulitzers and McKay's now serve as kiosks for a variety of gifts and collectables.

The Jekyll Island Museum works diligently to preserve the irreplaceable properties located throughout the historic district, with proceeds from the museum's gift shop serving to help them continue their mission of preservation. While you're in the gift shop, make sure to check out the rest of the displays and media located throughout the museum.

Hours of Operation

Open daily from 9 a.m. to 5 p.m.

————

Jekyll Books at the Old Infirmary
101 Old Plantation Road, Jekyll Island, Georgia 31527
(912) 635-3077

Originally dubbed the Furness Cottage, built by Frank Furness in 1890, Jekyll books at the Old Infirmary has a long, storied history. Not long after the cottage was sold to Joseph Pulitzer, the Victorian homestead was purchased by the Goodyear family, who eventually donated it to the Jekyll Island Club for use as an infirmary.

Now the property serves as Jekyll's prime bookstore, housing a variety of popular fiction and non-fiction while differentiating itself from mainstream book retailers by featuring an abundance of local literature covering every genre imaginable. Travel guides and coffee table books focusing on Georgia's picturesque coast from Tybee Island down to Cumberland's shores are plentiful in the store, along with books about ghost stories, southern legends, and works from locally and nationally renowned authors fill the shelves from top to bottom.

If you're a bona fide book lover, you'll want to spend some time perusing this store. When you visit, don't forget to make your way up the narrow staircase to the second floor, where even more literary works await.

Hours of Operation

Monday through Saturday from 10 a.m. to 5 p.m.
Sundays from 11 a.m. to 5 p.m.

———

Just by Hand
29 Pier Road, Jekyll Island, Georgia 31527
(912) 635-9810
www.shopjustbyhand.com

Looking for authentically handcrafted gifts to take home? Then look no further than Just by Hand, Jekyll's exclusive all-handcrafted gift gallery. Everything in their gallery is one of a kind, crafted by talented artists and made to inspire.

Just by Hand offers a wide selection of wall art such as paintings and photographs showcasing southern coastal scenes to choose from, as well as artwork formed from earthlier elements such as pottery, metals, woodworks and glass. They also provide an array of gifts like soaps, nesting dolls, ornaments, candles, jewelry, and games.

Few things compare to gifting a handcrafted item. If you're looking for something thoughtful and unique to take home to a loved one, consider stopping by Just by Hand, located in the Jekyll Island Historic District.

Hours of Operation

Open daily from 10 a.m. to closing *(times vary by season)*

———

The Bare Necessities

Other stores, shops and markets outside of Jekyll's historic district are scattered across the island, offering a wide variety of groceries, camping supplies, beach gear, clothing, media, artwork, and more. Whether you left your golf shirt at home and need a replacement before hitting the links, or you're just looking to pick up the makings of a great cocktail to take back to your hotel room or island outpost, finding the bare necessities on Jekyll Island is a synch.

———

Jekyll Island Market and Deli
11 Main Street, Jekyll Island, Georgia 31527
(912) 635-2253
www.jekyllmarket.com

Jekyll Island Market and Deli has served the residents and visitors of Jekyll Island for almost half a century. Conveniently located in Jekyll's new Beach Village, this local market open 7 days a week provides patrons with the freshest meats, vegetables, gourmet items, sweets, coffee, frozen drinks and more.

Be sure to check out the market's boardwalk deli. There you'll find your favorite deli sandwiches handcrafted with premium ingredients made just the way you like them. Jekyll Market also has a self-service salad bar open every day from 11 a.m. to 7 p.m. You can find out more by visiting their website at www.jekyllmarket.com or calling the number above.

Hours of Operation

Sunday through Thursday from 8 a.m. to 8 p.m.
Friday and Saturday from 8 a.m. to 9 p.m.

———

Jekyll Island Beverage Center
31 Ocean Way #103, Jekyll Island, GA 31527
(912) 635-2080

If you're looking for a package store on Jekyll Island, this is the only one you're going to find—at least for now. The Jekyll Island Beverage Center is exactly what you would expect from the island's only package store: mainstream beer with a few craft brews, wines, cigars, and a wide variety of liquor brands and spirits.

For those preferring the hard stuff on the rocks, the store always has plenty of ice in stock, along with some soft drinks and mixers for adult-beverage connoisseurs that like to stir things up a bit. Jekyll Island Beverage Center has everything you need to stay cool and relax after a long day of sightseeing and beachcombing on the island.

Store hours have been seasonal in the past, so keep that in mind before stopping by. If you're concerned about running into closed doors before your personal cocktail hour, be sure to call ahead.

Hours of Operation

Monday through Thursday from 10 a.m. to 8 p.m.
Friday and Saturday from 10 a.m. to 9 p.m.
Sundays from 12 p.m. to 6 p.m.

———

Flash Foods
50 Ben Fortson Parkway, Jekyll Island, GA 31527
(912) 635-2244

Open 24 hours a day, 7 days a week, Flash Foods on Jekyll is your go-to source for late-night cravings and last-minute necessities before heading to your final destination. Located on the left just across the M.E. Thompson Memorial Bridge right next to Dairy Queen, Flash Foods has what you need to keep your gas tanked topped off, too, offering both unleaded and diesel gasoline at competitive prices.

Flash Foods has everything you would expect from a typical inland convenience store, along with other items indicative of an island destination, including beach balls, volley balls, boogie boards, beach towels, sunscreen and kids toys. With a convenient location and proximity to DQ, this should be your first stop before making your way further into the island. Fill up your tank, grab some snacks and get to the beach!

* * * * *

RECREATION

Whether going on a long vacation or simply jetting off for the weekend, we all look for different ways to pass the time. Some travelers are content with sitting on the beach all day, while others need to fill their itineraries with exciting activities from dawn till dusk.

If the latter category sounds like you, then this is your section. Between seaside golfing and saltwater fishing, to river kayaking, biking and trail hiking, Jekyll Island hosts a plethora of outdoor coastal activities to keep the most restless wonderers occupied and entertained.

***

Biking on Jekyll Island

One look at Jekyll Island's gorgeous bicycle trails, and you'll think the island itself was created solely to accommodate two-wheeling bike enthusiasts. There are over 20 miles of bike trails on Jekyll that encompass the entire island, leading peddlers down paths shaded by thick maritime canopies, through breezy marshlands steeped in sea-salt air, winding through the sand dunes and down the beaches of Jekyll's Atlantic coast.

One of the best things about Jekyll's bike trails is their diversity. Looking to get a little sun while taking in oceanfront vistas? Then check out Jekyll's Ocean Views path, a 2-mile pedal that runs parallel to Jekyll's coastline. Would you rather explore Jekyll's maritime forests? Then consider the South Loop Trail, approximately 6 miles of bike path that starts at Ben Fortson Parkway, makes its way down to St. Andrews Picnic Area before heading back through the shade trees along South Riverview Drive.

Other paths include the Historic District route, the North Loop, and the Golf Course route, featuring wide-angle views of the best golf that Jekyll Island has to offer. You can pick up a free map detailing Jekyll's many bike paths by stopping by the guest information center at the tollbooth on your way onto the island, or at the bike rental location in the brick building right next to Jekyll Island Mini Golf at the corner of North Beachview Drive and Shell Road (from Beachview, turn onto Shell Road, entrance is up 100 yards on your right).

We prefer the physical maps available at the two locations cited above. If you would like to download a .pdf version of Jekyll Island's bike paths to your smartphone or tablet, be sure to visit www.goldenisles.com.

Bicycle Rentals

Did you leave the bikes at home? No worries, Jekyll Island has several bike rental options, with many locations offering hourly, daily and weekly rates. Whether you're looking to spend the entire day meandering down Jekyll's many bike trails, or would like to get in an hour or two of two-wheeled exercise before dinner, the locations below will be happy to accommodate you.

Beachside Bike Rentals
60 South Beachview Drive, Jekyll Island, GA 31527
(912) 635-9801
www.beachsidebikerentals.com

Located at the Days Inn and Suites on South Beachview Drive. The bike rental shack can be spotted from the road on the north side of the hotel.

Hours of Operation

Open daily from 10 a.m. to 5 p.m., even during the offseason (weather permitting).

————

Mini-Golf Bike Rentals

Corner of North Beachview Drive and Shell Road, Jekyll Island, GA 31527
(912) 635-2648

You can't miss the bike rental barn located right next to Jekyll's only mini-golf course. This centrally located rental shop has it all. Whether you're looking to hop on a mini-surrey or dual trike with that special someone, or would rather go it alone on a traditional bicycle or a low-riding single-person trike, you can find them all here.

Popular rates include half-day bike rentals just under $6, with full days setting you back around $14 per person. Dual trikes and mini-surreys are rented by the hour, and cost between $16 and $20. You can bike the entire north loop at a leisurely pace in about two hours, so keep that in mind when determining how much your bike-rental excursion will set you back.

Hours of Operation

10 a.m. to 4 p.m. during the busy season. Hours vary during the offseason and during inclement weather.

————

Bike Rentals at the Jekyll Island Club Hotel

371 Riverview Drive, Jekyll Island, GA 31527
(855) 219-7338
www.jekyllclub.com

Looking to pick up a set of wheels closer to the historic district? By renting your bikes from the Jekyll Island Club Hotel, you'll be right in the thick of it; just keep in mind that you're going to pay a little extra for downtown convenience. According to the club's website, half day bike rentals are $10 per person, and full day rentals cost $18. The price difference may not matter much for yourself or another person, but if you're planning on taking the whole family out for a ride, then you may want to consider renting bikes closer to the beach.

Bike rentals at the Jekyll Island Club Hotel are available through the front desk.

***

Jekyll Island: An Equestrian Destination

Many visitors to Jekyll don't realize how much the island caters to horse lovers until they've already arrived. One trip to the island's northern end could showcase horseback riders enjoying afternoon strolls atop Appaloosas and Tennessee Walkers, or it may be the Arabians, palominos and paint geldings of Three Oaks Farms you spot winding through wooded horse trails and along coastal marshlands.

Horse sightings aren't limited to the northern end, either, as the historic district is home to some of the most enchanting island carriage rides you'll encounter at a tourist destination. Carriage tours come in several varieties as well, from peaceful evening tours that allow you to take in the historic district with a loved one with the sounds of hooves clacking along the oyster-shell streets filling the salt air, or narrated historic carriage rides that offers a provocative history lesson while riding past the previous homes of Rockefellers, Goodyears, and Pulitzers.

Although visitors have the option of bringing their own horses, or obtaining equestrian services from a variety of different vendors across the South's Atlantic coast, we highly recommend taking advantage of the wonderful equestrian services that Three Oaks Farm has to offer.

Three Oaks Farm is a local business established close to Jekyll Island in nearby Brunswick, Georgia, and is the leading provider of equestrian services for Jekyll Island, St. Simons Island and Sea Island.

Three Oaks Farm is proud to provide visitors of Jekyll Island with several options for enjoying a day full of coastal sunshine and affable equines. Their wide variety of equestrian services is listed below:

Three Oaks Farm Equestrian Services

100 Stable Road, Jekyll Island, Georgia 31527
(912) 635-9500
www.threeoaksfarm.org

If galloping alongside the crashing ocean surf of the Atlantic is on your bucket list, then you can easily check this one off during your next visit to Jekyll, along with exploring a maritime forest and trotting through marshlands on horseback.

Three Oaks Farms offers several different riding options catering to your specific needs and designed to work around your busy vacation schedule. Whether you're single and looking for some beachside seclusion atop your trusty steed, or would like to get the family together for a group outing, Three Oaks Farm is there to accommodate.

All prices are valid as of January 1st 2016 and are subject to change.

Horse Rentals

1 Hour Beach Ride
      Public Group Ride $58
      Private Ride $100

1.5 Hour Beach Ride
      Public Group Ride $68
      Private Ride $125

3 Hour Beach and Forest Ride
      Public Group Ride $165
      Private Ride $265

Sunset Beach Ride
      Public Group Ride $78
      Private Ride $135
1.5 Hour Sunset Beach Ride

| Public Group Ride | $88 |
| Private Ride | $145 |

1 Hour Swim Rides
| Public | $98 |
| Private | $155 |

1 Hour Moonlight Rides
| Public | $88 |
| Private | $145 |

Carriage Rides

Daytime Carriage Tour: $15 adults, $7 children ages 4 to 12. Kids 3 and under are free.
Private Evening Carriage Tour: $40 for two people, $15 additional adults, $7 for children ages 4 to 12. Kids 3 and under are free.

Private Evening Cinderella Carriage Tour: $50 for two people, $15 additional adults, $7 for children ages 4 to 12. Kids 3 and under are free.

Narrated Historic Tour and Tea: $40 per adult, $20 children ages 4 to 12. Kids 3 and under are free.

Haywagon Rides

1 Hour Haywagon Ride ($50 for each additional hour): $275

Pony Rides

1 Hour Pony Rides ($50 for each additional hour): $475

Portable Petting Zoo

2 Hour Portable Petting Zoo ($50 for each additional hour): $475

Kids' Camps

Kids camp options vary, with most programs revolving around local families that are available to drop their kids off throughout the year. For families visiting Jekyll Island, Three Oaks Farm has a kids camp program that was designed specifically with vacationing families in mind.

Vacation Day Camp: $75 per day, with each additional child ½ off.

Schedule and availability can be checked through www.Zerve.com/threeoaks. Booking in advance is highly recommended. You can also schedule appointments over the phone by calling Zerve at (912) 266-8116. Camp bookings are asked to call Three Oaks Farms directly at (912) 635-9500.

Three Oaks Farm Equestrian Services Brunswick location is at 332 Oyster Road, Brunswick, Georgia 31523. Contact: threeoaksfarm1@aol.com.

***

Golfing on Jekyll Island

For a relatively small island, Jekyll Island features several golf courses should the links start calling your name. Below is an extensive list of your golfing options on the island.

Jekyll Island Golf Club
322 Captain Wylly Road, Jekyll Island, Georgia 31527
(912) 635-2368 or (912) 635-3464

Jekyll Island Golf Club is the only golf resort located on Jekyll Island, featuring four separate courses and 63 holes to play. These courses range from wide-open fairways and short green shots to dogleg obstacles and perilous sand traps, creating a challenging atmosphere for both high handicappers and scratch players alike.

The course also hales itself as the largest public golf resort in the state of Georgia, and while private club members may raise an eyebrow to public courses, don't let the easy access fool you: Jekyll Island is a conservationist's dream, taking pride in every square inch of its property.

The Jekyll Island Golf Club is no different, and strives to provide golfers with the best golfing experiences possible–just don't expect them to go fishing your golf balls out of the water hazards.

Rates are comparable to many mainland golf courses in Georgia: expect to pay $55 for 18 holes of primetime golf with a cart rental, and $32 if you plan on walking (2016 rates are listed below, and are subject to change at any time). Twilight rates are substantially lower after 2 p.m., and considering you'll be teeing off over the flat fairways of the East Coast, you should have no trouble getting in 18 holes after two o'clock during the summer months, although you'd be pushing it in the winter. (Late December/early January sunsets are around 5:30 p.m. on Jekyll.)

Let's check out Jekyll's four courses to see what sets each one apart from the rest. Any one of these courses is sure to provide plenty of memorable moments during your next golfing excursion.

———

Great Dunes
(912) 635-2170
Great Dunes has a separate phone number and rates from the three 18-hole courses. Call ahead with inquiries.

The first and only 9-hole golf course on the island, the historic Great Dunes course is a relic of Jekyll Club affluence. Completed in 1926, the course was the brainchild of famed course architect Walter Travis, who was summoned by Rockefeller and company to create the finest course imaginable. Needless to say, money was no object at the time.

The result was a 9-hole course set amongst beach views, windswept sand dunes, oak trees and the subtropical warmth that makes Great Dunes course a pleasantly comfortable choice for a golf outing any time of year. Great Dunes remains in the same condition it was some 90 years ago, making a round on this coastal course an event like no other.

If you're an avid golfer, make sure you cross this piece of history off your bucket list by taking a morning or afternoon walk across same links graced by oil tycoons, railroad magnets, and the wealthiest Americans alive during the Roaring Twenties.

———

Indian Mound

If you're looking to snag 18 holes during your next golf outing, but you want to keep distance covered to a minimum, then consider playing Indian Mound. Indian Mound is the shortest of the Jekyll's three separate 18-hole courses, yet delivers an enjoyable outing with each and every available yard.

The course is considered a forgiving one, with many wide-open fairways and an open layout welcomed by high handicappers and golf enthusiasts suffering from occasional hooks and slices. Scoring opportunities abound at Indian Mound, so if you're looking to turn in the best score possible, this course is a great place to start.

———

Oleander

Myriad challenges await you on the Oleander course, which is considered by many to be the most difficult course at the resort. According to clubhouse chatter, this course is one of the local favorites on the island, and for good reason; many club members hone their game daily, and Oleander delivers the most obstacles out of the four courses on Jekyll. Tight tree-lined fairways, inland water hazards, sand-trap-guarded greens and sharp bends make Oleander the course for golfers seeking a formidable challenge.

Oleander is also considered the course to play for wildlife enthusiasts. Not only are you bound to see plenty of whitetail deer grazing and coastal birds drifting in the breeze, you may even spot an alligator or two taking in a little sun near one of the many water hazards. There was also once a large Osprey nest near one of the holes on Oleander, so don't be surprised if you see these magnificent predatory birds soaring high while seeking out an inland freshwater meal.

———

Pine Lakes

Pine Lakes is the last of four courses at Jekyll Island Golf Club, and is the longest of the four courses at the resort. Playing 18 holes at Pine Lakes takes golfers through forests consisting of longstanding southern pines with palms and palmettos interweaving amongst the forest canopy.

Plenty of straight shots and long fairways make this course the most family friendly of the four at the golf resort. Tee boxes are widespread between pro boxes and junior tees, giving golfers both young and old an equal advantage when hitting the links. If you're interested in taking your future golf pros on an 18-round excursion at the heart of Jekyll Island, then Pine Lakes golf course is the one for you.

———

2016 Popular Rates

Rates are subject to change at the club's discretion. Call ahead with questions and inquiries.

Great Dunes Rates *(Jekyll's only 9-hole course)*

With cart: $25
Walking: $15

18 Hole Course Rates Regular Hours

With cart: $55 ($29 ages 15 and under)
Walking: $32 ($18 ages 15 and under)

18 Hole Twilight Rates *(after 2 p.m.)*

With cart: $35
Walking: $20

———

Mini Golf with The Kids

Jekyll Island Mini Golf
At the corner of North Beachview Drive and Shell Road.
(912) 635-2648

Who doesn't like miniature golf? Jekyll Island Mini Golf is the island's enduring putt-putt park located right next door to Red Bug Motors Pizza and Pub. Not much has changed since we first made our way there back in the 1980s, and the grounds remain a nostalgic cornerstone for any longtime visitors to the island.

Jekyll Island Mini Golf has two different courses to play on, so be sure to switch it up a little if the kids insist on playing putt-putt two days in a row. The convenient location is across the street from the new Tortuga Jacks, and right next door to Red Bug Motors Pizza.

Rates

$6.08 per game. If you're staying for the week, you may consider buying a 3-game ticket for $15. For frequent flyers, they even offer a 10-gamer for $45.

Hours of Operation

9 a.m. to 7 p.m. during the busy season. Hours vary during the offseason and during inclement weather.

***

Tennis

Jekyll Island Tennis Center
400 Captain Wylly Road, Jekyll Island, Georgia 31527
(912) 635-3154

Looking for the kind of love involving rackets, nets, and bouncy yellow tennis balls? Then look no further than the Jekyll Island Tennis Center, a 13-court center where you can hone your tennis skills by bringing a friend, getting in on a pickup game arranged by the staff, testing your mettle against a tennis-ball machine, or trying your hand at table tennis in the main building.

One of the main features of Jekyll's tennis center that makes it unique from most others is the fact that the courts are made of clay, as opposed to concrete or asphalt. Clay courts result in slower ball speeds, helping players focus on their form and efficiency. Taking advantage of Jekyll's clay tennis courts will give you an advantage over your tennis buddies back home, considering you'll have time to work on your strategy while perfecting your muscle memory before speeding things up back on the asphalt.

Rates

Tennis center rates are pretty straightforward: $8 a person per session for court fees, with an extra $3 per session to rent a racket. You can pick up a ball hopper for $5 a session, and a ball machine for $12 an hour. Locker rentals, racket-stringing services, and tennis clinics are also available. Call for inquiries.

Hours of Operation

The full-service pro shop is open every day from 9 a.m. to 6 p.m., but don't let the 9-hour day deter you: if you want to hit the courts later in the evening, or even at night during those steaming summer months, you can book after 6 by calling ahead and making a reservation.

***

Island Fishing

Jekyll Island is a saltwater angler's paradise, simply because there are so many species in a multitude of habitats just waiting to get hooked. Over eight miles of Atlantic coastline, mazes of inland salt marshes, shallow flats, and estuaries put the island in prime saltwater fishing territory.

Several fishing charters are available for those seeking the adrenalin rush of an offshore adventure on the high seas while searching for grouper, wahoo, barracuda, king mackerel, amberjacks and sharks, or you can opt to find a quiet spot on one of Jekyll's secluded shores and surf-cast for a variety of saltwater species including redfish, speckled trout, triple tail and cobia.

Regulations and licensing

Because many rules and regulations regarding Georgia fishing change annually, we recommend visiting www.gofishgeorgia.com for the most accurate and up-to-date fishing regulations and general licensing information for Jekyll Island.

To view fishing license rates for residents and non-residents, you can visit www.georgiawildlife.com. If you would like to skip all the bologna and head straight for the web portal to purchase your fishing license online, visit www.gooutdoorsgeorgia.com. There you can purchase or reprint your state fishing license by entering your account information. Don't worry if you don't already have an account; you can create a new one through the web portal.

If you're new to fishing in Georgia, the state Department of Natural Resources has released an excellent guide covering Georgia sport fishing regulations for 2016. This guide details license requirements, saltwater fish measuring tips, popular saltwater fish illustrations, information, and more. You can access the digital edition of the fishing guide by visiting www.eregulations.com/georgia/fishing/.

Where can I buy my license in person?

If you're already on the island and you don't want to take a trip into Brunswick, then you've got one choice:

Maxwell's General Store in the new Beach Village at the roundabout connecting Ben Fortson with North and South Beachview Drive. Maxwell's can also hook you up with fishing supplies while you're there. Hours vary but are typically 9 a.m. to 6 p.m. in the offseason, staying open later during busy months.

10 Main Street, Jekyll Island, Georgia 31527
Phone: (912) 635-2205

If you're making a trip to Brunswick—or coming through on your way to the island—then you can pick up a fishing license at either Dick's Sporting Goods or Wal-Mart.

Dick's Sporting Goods
440 Glynn Isle, Brunswick, Georgia 31525
(912) 262-2433

Wal-Mart Brunswick
150 Altama Connector, Brunswick, Georgia 31525
(912) 261-1616

The Georgia Department of Natural Resources office in Brunswick has more information regarding locations where you can purchase a license. Their number is 912-264-7218.

If you live in Georgia and want to purchase a license in-person before heading to Jekyll, check out the "find a licensing agent" portal by visiting www.georgiawildlife.org/LicenseAgents.

Although rules are always subject to change, there are some regulations that are generally accepted, but it's always a good idea to check the state's website prior to wetting a hook.

Anglers 15 and under do not require a license – but if you can drive a car without your parents riding shotgun, then you'll need to purchase a Georgia fishing license to go along with that shiny new driver's permit.

Georgia licenses require SIP permit to fish the coast – If you already have a Georgia fishing license covering freshwater fishing, then you won't have to chock up more cash to wet a hook in the salty seas, but you'll still need to obtain a free Saltwater Information Program (SIP) permit to fish Georgia's saltwater shores.

Most charters have licenses covering guests – If you're booking a charter, you may not need to purchase a Georgia fishing license. Make sure you check with your specific charter company before assuming you'll be covered under the charter's license.

I've got my license, now what?

Have your Georgia fishing license, but unsure where to go from here? You may think for a moment that taking the same zoom worms and the Zebco 33 fishing rod you use in the freshwater streams and ponds back home may suffice, but saltwater fishing Jekyll's waters is a little different.

If you are looking to be your own guide during your time fishing Jekyll's assorted inlets, streams and beaches, then we'd like to give you a few quick pointers first.

The size of your fishing rod matters. Taking your son's 3-foot Mickey Mouse pole into waist-deep water and casting into the surf is probably going to result in a broken rod and one upset kid. Overkill works the other way, too, and hauling the 10-foot deep-sea pole to the local fishing pier is likely to draw a few snickers from neighboring anglers as you struggle to hoist your catch up vertically from the waters far below.

When it comes to choosing a saltwater fishing pole, exactly where you plan to fish is an important deciding factor. There are three types of fishing poles we're going to recommend, all for three very different saltwater fishing situations:

Surf fishing rods – This is the type of rod you'll want if you plan on fishing right off the beach. Surf fishing rods should be long enough to assist in casting past the breakers, so look for one anywhere from seven to ten feet in length. Saltwater is very corrosive and can destroy a rod and reel in just a few outings, so be sure to look for a rod with stainless steel guides, a lightweight aluminum reel, and corrosion-resistant parts e.g. a stainless bail wire for spinning reels. You'll also want a long-cast handle with comfortable foam grips to reduce slippage when wet.

Pier fishing rods – Fishing from a pier means you won't be reeling *in* fish so much as you'll be reeling them *up*, so you'd better have a rod that can handle the job. A good pier fishing rod should be medium-heavy to heavy, and can be anywhere from six to nine feet in length, although you'll probably want to go with a shorter stick since you're not really casting for distance off the pier to begin with. Several name brands like Shakespeare and Ugly Stik sell pier fishing combo packs for around $50 and include pre-spooled line, artificial bait for shallow-water feeders and pre-tied rigs.

Another pier-fishing consideration to make is a pier-fishing cart. Designed with the serious pier fishermen and women in mind, these two-wheeled carts allow you to haul your cooler, bait, rods, reels and tackle to and from your favorite pier with ease. If you're thinking about buying a cart, make sure it has wheels big enough to handle sandy beaches, too.

Offshore fishing rods – Offshore rods, also called deep-sea rods, are designed for monster catches: we're talking sailfish, wahoo, amberjacks, triggerfish, marlin and sharks. Deep-sea guides typically go with graphite due to their massive strength. If you're planning on booking a charter with the offshore experts listed below, don't worry about shopping for a good deep-sea rod, as those will be provided for you on your charter-fishing trip.

What kind of bait should I use?

Hitting an Appalachian trout stream with little more than can of corn and some red wigglers is probably enough to attract the stocked rainbow trout, but it won't get you too far in the Atlantic. Different fish in different ecosystems have different tastes, and the saltwater fish residing in Jekyll's waters are no different.

So what should you be loading your hook with on the coast? It depends on what you want to catch. Below is a list of popular bait and what you can expect to lure in on each.

Cut bait – A must for any newbie saltwater angler just getting his or her feet wet, cut bait is a solid choice for fishers seeking quick bites in Jekyll's waters. The reason cut bait is so effective around Jekyll Island is simple: Jekyll's waters tend to be rather murky year round, making it hard for predatory fish to identify meals with eyesight alone.

Instead of luring fish in by the sight of a shiny spinner or artificial lure, cut bait lures them in with smell, ensuring nearby ocean predators know exactly where your bait is without having to actually see it. Cut bait works on a variety of ocean-dwelling fish, from speckled trout and bluefish to bottom feeders like catfish, grouper and carp.

Shrimp – Shrimp is a great alternative to cut bait, doing much of the same work with little to no effort. Simply load up your hook, cast away and wait for a bite. Some anglers actually sight-cast shrimp toward fish while trolling in shallow inland waters and near structures in the Jekyll River. Tripletail love shrimp, and redfish are natural bottom feeders, so entrees like shrimp are right up their alley.

Dough balls – Many coastal fish respond to dough balls in the same manner they do to other bottom-feeding lures such as shrimp, crab and baitfish. Dough balls are especially popular for reeling in big catfish, both in freshwater and saltwater environments. The fact that dough balls are rather clean and don't smell make them a great alternative to cut bait.

Artificial lures – Coming in endless varieties designed to attract the most hesitant of saltwater fish, artificial lures can help you trick a fish into instinctively hitting your line, all without the mess of live bait. Plastic minnow striper plugs, wooden belly swimmers, live bait metal jigs and diamond drone spoons are just as fun to call out as Joe Dirt's list of essential fireworks, and can pack an explosive punch in the water, too.

There's a bucketful of artificial lures out there designed to attract every type of fish, so it's best to determine what you'll be fishing for and what's in season before heading to the bait shop. Most artificial lures sold individually specify the target species right there on the label, so they'll be no question as to the saltwater fish each lure was made to attract.

Where can I go fishing on my own?

Prefer a little solitude when you're casting a line? When it comes to fishing Jekyll, you've got plenty of options. Miles of beaches are perfect for surfcasting–just don't forget the sunscreen (we'd stick with a minimum SPF 50). You may even consider taking an umbrella and a beach cart loaded with food and drinks if you're going to be making a day of it. At the very least, you should take plenty of water, a big hat and a bucket (preferably with a seat top) for your equipment if you're going to be hitting the surf to test your skills past the breakers.

Southbound – Worried about swimmers, or just looking for a little isolation? Consider breaking away from the main beaches and head south toward South Dunes Park. There you can park and take the boardwalk to the beach, away from bustling hotel beachfronts and the popular Great Dunes Beach Access. The southernmost end of Jekyll at St. Andrews Picnic Area is also another great alternative for anglers seeking peace and quiet.

Toward the north – Options range from inland stream fishing at Clam Creek Picnic Area, to fishing Jekyll Sound from the Clam Creek fishing pier. There you'll also find Jekyll Island Fishing Center, where you can stock up on live bait, supplies, snacks, and even book a charter trip.

If you decide to park at the Clam Creek Picnic Area, you'll have several choices that should guarantee at least a little seclusion. As you drive in you'll see Clam Creek to your right. There are several creek access points right from the banks, so just pick out a spot and let your lures fly. If creek fishing isn't your thing, there's always sound fishing at the pier, or you can take a stroll northeast across the Clam Creek Bridge toward Jekyll's northernmost beach. Here you'll find views of Saint Simons Island to the north while fishing the salty waters of Driftwood Beach.

The old Jekyll Island Bridge – There's one spot that's a favorite for local pier-fishing fanatics, and it's the old bridge at Jekyll Island. The new M.E. Thompson Memorial Bridge crossing over the Jekyll River didn't exist until the mid-90s, preceded by the old drawbridge that lies in the shadows to the north of the new causeway.

Since its conversion into a fishing pier, the drawbridge has been removed, which now divides this centrally located bridge-turned-fishing pier into two sections: one section is located on the left side of Jekyll Island Road/GA 520 E right before you cross the main bridge to get to the island, while the other section is accessed on the island side on old Jekyll Island Road (toward the historic district). To get to the old bridge on the island side, you'll take a left after crossing the new bridge onto Riverview Drive, then another immediate left, driving parallel to M.E. Thompson Memorial Bridge on Jekyll Island Road.

Need more information on the vast fishing opportunities on Jekyll Island? Contact any one of the locations below for details on local fishing, tips, charters and more.

Jekyll Harbor Marina
1 Harbor Road, Jekyll Island, Georgia 31527
(912) 635-3137

———

Jekyll Island Fishing Center – Fishing Pier
10 Clam Creek Road, Jekyll Island, Georgia 31527
(912) 270-7474

———

Fishing Charters

No idea where the fish are biting? Perhaps you don't have a taste for brackish stream trout and marsh-dwelling reds, and you'd rather be reeling in massive mackerels, barracuda and wahoo known to reside miles offshore instead. If the latter is the case, then you'll need a guide to get you there and back again, which is exactly why hiring a qualified fishing charter is a must.

Several fishing charters operate out of Jekyll Island, with many of them licensed for saltwater fishing (meaning you don't have to purchase a license yourself) as well as certified as professional fishing charters by the U.S. Coast Guard.

The following guides are the "reel" deal, and are guaranteed to put you on the fish, whether you're trolling inshore, hitting up nearby rivers and estuaries, or heading miles offshore in search of epic battles with the rulers of the deep blue sea.

———

Coastal Expeditions
(912) 270-3526
www.coastalcharterfishing.com

Captain Eric Moody has been fishing coastal Georgia his entire life. A ten-year resident of Jekyll, Captain Moody has an extensive knowledge of the vast waters and varying ecosystems surrounding Georgia's gem, and will be sure to deliver an exceptional fishing excursion regardless of what you're after.

Coastal Expeditions isn't restricted to fishing, either. Aside from inshore and offshore fishing trips—full days and half days—they also specialize in dolphin and sightseeing tours around Jekyll's unique coastal waters. Be sure to ask about sightseeing trips to neighboring Cumberland Island: there's nothing quite like drifting along and spotting a few of Cumberland's feral horses while floating down the Intracoastal Waterway.

———

Offshore Charters
(912) 270-7474

Let Captain Larry Crews take you and yours on an offshore fishing trip you won't soon forget. Climb aboard one of three boats helmed by Crews and company as they take you out to sea in search of tarpon, tripletail, trout and reds.

Offshore Charters also books shark-fishing trips–at night. If you thought catching these cartilaginous creatures was exciting during the daytime, imagine what it'll be like hooking these bad boys surrounded by the glow of a moonlit ocean. These trips stayed booked up, so make sure you call well ahead of your desired charter date.

———

Southeastern Angling
(877) 605-3474
www.captainscottowens.com

Located off Saint Simons Island to the north of Jekyll, Captain Scott Owens has no problem bringing boat and gear down to Jekyll Harbor Marina to pick you up for an incredible fishing journey across Georgia's Golden Isles. Both Captain Owens and Captain Rob Aldridge are full-time fishing guides specializing in light tackle and fly fishing along the southeastern seaboard.

Their fleet of center consoles, bay boats, and skiffs are ready to take you anywhere from serene tidal marshes to the fury of the wide-open ocean in search of big bites and high seas adventure. These guys spend every day on the waters surrounding Saint Simons, Jekyll, Cumberland, and northern Florida. They have the experience to get you there and back safely, while landing you on some formidable fish in the process.

———

Captain Mark Noble
(912) 634-1219
www.georgiafishing.net

Operating out of the St. Simons Fishing Center to the north of Jekyll, Captain Noble has spent his entire life on the waters surrounding Jekyll Island, and has a reputation for landing fish when everyone else is coming up short.

Captain Noble runs a full-service fishing charter, meaning he can get you anywhere from inland shallows to deep offshore waters. If you're into monster fish, then you have to check out his website at georgiafishing.net. There you'll see the kind of bull reds and tarpon Noble and crew haul in on a regular basis. Captain Noble's all about family, too, so feel free to bring the kids along, regardless of experience.

***

Hiking

Paths, Trails and Trajectories on Jekyll Island

Jekyll Island certainly has its fair share of bike paths and walking trails. In fact, over 20 miles of paved pathways, gravel walkways, and downtrodden paths wind through and around Jekyll Island. If you're looking for a place to take the bikes, don't forget to check out our section titled, "Biking on Jekyll Island."

But if you're looking for an excursion off the beaten path, you won't find a map for your next adventure at the welcome center. Several hiking trails cut through the marshlands and maritime forests of Jekyll Island, giving subtropical explorers a firsthand look at what it must have been like to step foot on the island long before developers made their mark.

Many of these hidden hiking trails are not well marked, making it difficult for those unfamiliar with the area to take advantage of these secluded footpaths. That's why we've highlighted key landmarks for hikers to be on the lookout for when venturing into Jekyll's backcountry.

A few things to keep in mind before hopping onto one of Jekyll's little-known nature trails: carry plenty of water, wear plenty of bug spray, bring your cell phone, and take mental notes of where you're at. If you don't feel comfortable diving deeper into Jekyll's maritime forests, just go back the way you came.

If you do get lost, stay calm and remember the following: Jekyll Island is only a mile and a half across at its widest point, with the seven-mile length of the island running north to south. In other words, as long as you're moving east or west, you've got a relatively short walk to the island's edge.

South End Trails

Located south of Ben Fortson Parkway, these southern trails take explorers off the beaten path and into a world little known to outsiders.

Grandfather Tree Loop Trail – If you don't know exactly how to get to Grandfather Tree Trail from South Beachview Drive, odds are you'll drive right by it. Unmarked with a tight entrance lined with saw palmettos and shaded by southern hardwoods, the Grandfather Tree Loop is a quarter-mile hike through Jekyll's maritime-forest interior.

So why is it called Grandfather Tree Loop? Because at the center of the trail lies what's known to locals as the Grandfather Tree. According to Jekyll4H.org, the tree is estimated to be over 150 years old, meaning this tree lucked out and avoided being axed for timber long before the island was protected. Solid limbs branching out from multiple points along

108

Grandfather Tree's massive trunk make getting a picture of the whole tree a challenge, so if you're looking to snap the embodiment of the grand southern live oak with your DSLR, make sure you bring a wide-angle lens.

How do you get to Grandfather Tree Loop Trail? The easiest route is via South Beachview Drive. You'll drive to the Jekyll Island Soccer Complex, paying close attention to the woods across the street from the complex. Park your car at the soccer complex, walk out of the complex and look directly across the street. The northernmost trailhead will be just to your right, about 2 o'clock. You'll see a power pole just to the right of the trailhead marking the point of entrance.

The trail comes out just over 200 yards south on South Beachview Drive, directly in front of the Jekyll Island 4H Center. Grandfather Tree Loop Trail isn't an epic hike, but don't let the short distance fool you: there's plenty of flora to see on the forest trail, including the occasional creepy crawlers (watch your step!) and a small marsh area about halfway through. Any true botanical enthusiast will want to take their time.

Southern Beachview-Riverview Connector – Just north of Grandfather Tree Loop Trail lies one of the easier-to-find Beachview-Riverview Connectors (there are three on the south side of the island). This trail serves as a cut-through between the southern portion of the island's two main drags, and will shave almost a mile and a half off your trip as opposed to following the main roads all the way south to the entrance of St. Andrews Picnic Area before looping back around toward the north.

Whereas Grandfather Tree Loop Trail is strictly for foot traffic only, the southernmost Beachview-Riverview Connector Trail has been well maintained to serve both foot traffic and bicycles. The only disclaimer is in regards to motorized vehicles of all kinds, none of which are allowed on the trail.

Finding this trail is simple. On the South Beachview Drive side, the trailhead is located 300 yards north of the Jekyll Island Soccer Complex entrance. If you're looking for it while heading south on Beachview, it's just under one-mile south of the Hampton Inn & Suites entrance on the right side of the road. Look for the sign at the trailhead pointing the way toward Riverview Drive.

South Dunes Park Beachview-Riverview Connector – If you're heading south on South Beachview Drive, the second connector trail is located just under 90 yards from the South Dunes Picnic Area entrance on the right side of the road. This connector trail linking Beachview and Riverview isn't marked with a sign, but is well maintained and in perfect shape for bicycle traffic. Be on the lookout for a green trashcan at the trailhead as you pass by—you can't miss it.

At 330 yards long, this is another quick cut-through if you're looking to shorten the length of your biking excursion. If you're hitting up the trail from Beachview, busting a right once you get to the end of the trail on the Riverview side will land you just half a mile south of the Summer Waves entrance on South Riverview Drive. Taking this cut-through instead of biking the entire way around the southern portion of the island on the main road will take two-and-a-half miles off your total ride.

Summer Waves Crossover Trail – 340 yards long and wide enough for the bikes, this trail is a great access point for the southern trails on Jekyll during the offseason. When Summer Waves Waterpark isn't going full force during the busy months (typically May through September) you can park your car in the empty parking lot, then shoot straight across the street to access the Summer Waves Crossover Trail. In as much time as it would take you to peddle across a football field, you'll be on South Beachview Drive less than half a mile south of the Days Inn and Suites.

At around 300 yards long each, these southern Beachview-Riverview Connector Trails can be breezed through in a matter of minutes, but they're also perfect for taking a moment to cool off under the forest canopy, especially when the sun's beating down on the main road. Next time you're biking or hiking down Jekyll's south end, give these cut-through trails a try.

South Riverview – Ben Fortson Connector Trail – There's a small stretch of road near the corners of South Riverview Drive and Ben Fortson Parkway near the island's center where the sidewalk/bike trail disappears into the woods for a cool 500 yards (0.3 miles). The winding bike trail features marsh, pond and creek views, as well as informative markers along the way.

You can hit up this short run on the bike or on foot by shooting straight across Ben Fortson Parkway from the Flash Foods on Jekyll. If you're on South Riverview Drive, the trailhead is 150 yards south of Harbor Road, and 300 yards from the intersection of South Riverview and Ben Fortson Parkway.

South Riverview Loop Trail – What's cool about some of the bike trails on Jekyll is the fact that many are impossible to miss. Just a quarter mile south of the Summer Waves entrance on South Riverview Drive lies the entrance to the South Riverview Loop Trail, a 0.9 mile stretch of interior bike path that takes riders across narrow bridges, pathways and marsh viewing areas with plenty of forest in between.

If you're coming from the north while heading south on South Riverview Drive, the loop trail is 0.35 miles south of Harbor Road on your left. This entrance also lies just over a tenth of a mile north of the entrance to Tidelands Nature Center. The trail intersects with the Summer Waves Crossover Trail at the halfway point.

Old Gun Carriage Trail – On the southern tip of Jekyll Island, tucked away behind a fortress of sand dunes and camouflaged by thick coastal forest, sits two hidden pieces of 19th century history few modern-day adventurers have laid eyes on: a pair of iron gun carriages positioned on Jekyll Island during the Spanish-American War. Just walking up on these wartime relics takes one back to another time and place, especially when considering their location deep in the south Jekyll woods.

Unlike many attractions on the island baring rich histories with plenty of attention to boot, these carriages have carried out a rather clandestine existence since their 1898 installment, situated behind high dunes overlooking passage between Jekyll and Cumberland Island.

Some of the history behind the gun carriages is unclear, but one reliable source of information comes directly from the National Geodetic Survey's website (A U.S. Coast and Geodetic Survey Mark is just a few feet away from the two gun carriages). A 1905 report detailing the condition of the area states:

"On the edge of the sand hills overlooking St. Andrews Sound at the southern end of Jekyll Island. The station is the center of a 4 in (sic) iron pivot at the center of a large square iron plate secured to the western one of two concrete gun platforms which were built during the Spanish War. The western halves of the platforms are somewhat broken and the two iron carriages are lying on their sides." – National Geodetic Survey, 1905.

Since that time, several reports have been filed in the National Geodetic Survey Database, with a 1965 report confirming the carriages had been turned upright and placed back on the pivots, which is accurate to this day.

As for the type of gun placed atop the carriages, getting absolute confirmation has been a challenge. During the course of our research, we found one promising forum dedicated to coastal artillery, www.cdsg.org, in which several members affirmed the carriages were designed for 10-inch Rodman guns (we will correct or confirm as soon as concrete information is made available.) In any case, these ironclad installments were meant to bear the weight of some serious artillery during a brief time of potential coastal conflict at the turn of the 20th century.

The challenge that lies with getting to the carriages has undoubtedly been the primary reason why this site has remained a coastal secret for some time. There are currently two trails leading to the site. The first trail beginning at St. Andrews Picnic Area is the longest, with difficulty depending on how much the undergrowth has taken over between busy seasons.

This trail is 0.40 miles, but it's no walk in the park. The trail can easily be lost, primarily because the heavily trodden deer paths intermingling with the main trail add to the confusion. Your best bet when hiking the St. Andrews portion is to look for the white blazes (paint stripes) about 5 feet up on trees meant to mark the appropriate trail.

If you're not interested in a long hike and just want to see the carriages, there is a much quicker route. Take South Beachview Drive (close to South River Drive) to Macy Lane. You'll pull into a residential area, and Macy Lane will dead end into St. Andrews Drive. There's a small area (clearing) you'll see past the stop sign; this is the entrance to the St. Andrews Cut Fire Control Road (walk a few yards in and you'll see the wooden sign).

At the sign, you'll notice a trail going up a steep incline and into the woods on the right–this is the trail to the carriages. Walk exactly 160 paces from the sign and you'll be in the midst of authentic Spanish-American War history, with two old war relics enjoying their retirement at the southern end of Jekyll Island.

Southern Point Trail – If you're looking to really get away from it all, Southern Point Trail is sure to lead the way to seclusion. From the St. Andrews Cut Fire Control Road sign (see Old Gun Carriage Trail directions) at the end of Macy Lane, continue straight past to hop on the poorly marked Southern Point Trail. Since this is another path that's difficult to navigate due to apparent trail spurs that lead to nowhere, it's important to take it in sections. And because your goal is to get to Jekyll's southernmost point, a good sense of direction also helps.

Beginning at the Fire Control Road sign, walk in a southeasterly direction for about 40 yards before veering left to stay on the sandy path. Look for a large, two-story residential house at the corner of Macy Lane and St. Andrews Drive (you'll have a clear view of the backyard). Your destination is straight back from this house, so keeping an eye on it for the first half is key.

About 50 yards directly behind the house, you'll find the worst boardwalk you've ever seen in your life. This 90-yard-long gator bait station is anything but welcoming, but we never said this path was for the faint at heart. Take your time walking the narrow footbridge, and when you get to the end you'll veer right toward 2 o'clock to stay on what's left of the trail.

At this point, a defined trail is hard to see, what with all the sand, but don't worry: at the end of the footbridge, you're only 140 yards from the dunes, so keep your eyes on the horizon, aim for the water and you'll be fine. Once you make it to the beach, break left toward the Atlantic Ocean and you'll be a quarter mile from the southern point of Jekyll Island. It's also not a bad idea to mark the spot you came off the trail and onto the beach at with something natural like a piece of driftwood or a handful of shells.

The southern point of Jekyll is rather secluded, so take extra care when venturing this far out. Don't be surprised if you see wildlife such as deer, osprey, and the occasional snake while traveling along this isolate corridor. Getting to Jekyll's secluded southern point is quite the endeavor, but if

you're up for an excursion that's truly off the beaten path, roll up your
sleeves and take a hike.

Southern Point to St. Andrews Park – Not a defined trail by any
means, but a great walk nonetheless. This one's easy: remember where the
Southern Point Trail hit the beach? (See above). Take a right instead of a
left, and head north along the beach toward St. Andrews Park and Picnic
Area.
This trajectory takes walkers on a 0.40-mile stroll up the southern tip of
Jekyll Island, with Jekyll Sound on your left and a magnificent view of
Cumberland Island just across the water.

John Cagle

***

116

North End Trails

These trails can be found north of Ben Fortson Parkway, and cover areas surrounding the historic district, the old Horton homestead, and Clam Creek.

Crane Road Trail – Connecting Ben Fortson Parkway with Stable Road, the Crane Road Trail takes hikers and bikers through a three-quarter mile stretch of marshlands and freshwater ponds, crossing streams while taking in wildlife viewing areas of the island interior. If you want a good shot at finding coastal birds, turtles, whitetail deer, or even a sunning alligator or two, this secluded inland trail is the one for you.

You can access the Crane Road Trail from two locations: the southern portion of the trail comes out at Ben Fortson Parkway, directly to the west side of the Flash Foods gas station. The northern trailhead dead-ends into Stable Road, just 20 yards south of the Shell Road intersection.

Major Horton Road Trail – This trail quite possibly represents the oldest established pathway cleared for travel by European settlers on Jekyll Island. Named for William Horton, a Major and trusted officer in James Oglethorpe's Georgia regiment, the road was originally cleared by Horton in the 1740s to connect his marsh-side estate with Jekyll's eastern beaches. Major Horton farmed much of the island, and this road was used to assist in his many agricultural endeavors, which included growing barley for producing the state's first beer.

The trailhead begins just a few yards to the north of the Horton House Ruins off North Riverview Drive, and runs 0.65 miles due east to its end at North Beachview Drive, across the street from Driftwood Bistro. (You'll run into a four-way intersection with another dirt road a quarter mile in; just keep moving forward and you'll be fine.)

Established as a road before being maintained for foot traffic, the Major Horton Road Trail has seen its fair share of growth and underbrush as the years have gone by, and with subtropical flora having a reputation for sprouting up and out in a hurry, don't be surprised if some portions of the trail are thicker than others. If you'd rather experience a shorter section of the trail, head west from the North Beachview side and turnaround at the freshwater pond to the south. Make sure to keep your eyes peeled for wildlife along the way.

Clam Creek Northern Loop Trail – This trail is a hybrid, mixing the asphalt pathways of the Clam Creek Bike Trail with the sandy beaches of Jekyll's northernmost shore. This 3-mile loop offers the best of both worlds, taking peddlers on a path through the inland Clam Creek wildlife viewing area, featuring marshland vistas, creek views, bird-nesting areas and raccoon country, before leading travelers along St. Simons Sound and across parts of Driftwood Beach.

There are two ways you can enjoy the Clam Creek Northern Loop Trail. From North Beachwood Drive, drive past the main Driftwood Beach parking area for 0.2 miles until you reach the north beach bird sanctuary trailhead on the right. (You'll see parking on the left, just enough room for four, maybe five cars at the most.) Park on the left, then head due east toward the beach. When your feet hit the shore, head north for 1.7 miles. The sand literally dead ends at the Clam Creek Bridge, where you can hop on the asphalt Clam Creek Bike Trail and head back south for 1.3 miles of comfortable walking. The bike trail dead ends into the short bird sanctuary trail, where busting a right (west) puts a mere 75 yards between you and your car.

If you'd rather depart from Clam Creek Picnic Area, cross the Clam Creek Bridge and hop onto the bike trail first, heading south. You'll take a left (east) on the bird-sanctuary trail, which dead ends at the beach, then make another left (north) for your stroll along the north shore, making the loop right back around to where you started some three miles earlier.

Old Amphitheater Trail –

By far the shortest "trail" to make the list, this little-known excursion is still worth every nature lover's time. Located on the east side of Stable Road near the Jekyll Island Fire Department, the Old Amphitheater Trail takes explorers to a decommissioned amphitheater in the middle of Jekyll's interior woods. The Amphitheater–haunting, weathered, and repossessed by the island's plants and animals–evokes an eerie feeling reminiscent to many once-bustling properties comprising Jekyll's historic district.

To get there, take the gravel drive called James Road, off Stable Road just 210 yards north of the Jekyll Island Fire Department (as of publication there was no road sign marking the gravel road on the east side of Stable Road, but you'll see James Road marked across Stable Road on the west side). 130 yards down James Road on the right you'll see a few places to park, as well as a trail breaking off marked by the old Amphitheater gateway sign; take that trail about 150 yards due east to the Amphitheater.

If you make your way to the abandoned Amphitheater, make sure you take the time to check out the old Amphitheater pond, located eastward behind the main stage of the arena. Several residents have spotted rare island inhabitants such as wood storks roosting in the trees surrounding the freshwater pond, so if you're into birding then this location is worth a look.

***

Kayaking

Local kayakers have dubbed the waters surrounding Jekyll as "Georgia's coastal trail system"—they're just not the kind of trails one finds on solid ground. You'll need to trade your hiking boots for a reliable boat to explore these trails, which extend inland from the northern beaches of Saint Simons Sound to the southern marshes dividing St. Andrews Picnic Area from neighboring Brunswick to the northwest.

These aquatic trails make up a vast system of coastal waterways, taking paddlers through a maze of brackish streams, rivers and marshes separating Jekyll from the mainland. It can be easy to lose one's bearings in unfamiliar waters, which is why we highly recommend taking a guide with you on your next kayaking adventure.

For us, there's only one kayaking guide servicing Jekyll Island to recommend: Southeast Adventure Outfitters.

Southeast Adventure Outfitters

313 Mallery Street, Saint Simons Island, Georgia 31522
(912) 638-6732 or (912) ME-TO-SEA
www.southeastadventure.com

Exploring the Georgia coast with visitors and locals alike since 1994, Southeast Adventure Outfitters is your one-stop-shop for kayak tours. Not only can they lead your family or group on tours through the waters surrounding Jekyll Island, but they also offer outings to other coastal islands such as Sapelo and Cumberland, as well as trips up and down the Altamaha and Satilla Rivers.

Southeast Adventure Outfitters offers both full and half-day tours, with shorter excursions perfect for testing out your sea legs. And if you decide you're completely hooked on kayaking altogether, you can check out their kayaks and standup paddleboards (SUP) they have for sale just right across the bridge from Jekyll at their Brunswick location.

Kayaking with Southeast will showcase the vast waters surrounding Jekyll from a perspective you never knew existed. We highly recommend booking your next kayaking excursion through these eco-friendly explorers.

***

Tours

Touring the island on foot is pretty fun, but diving deeper into the island's history, habitats, and scenery by taking a guided tour is sure to strengthen your appreciation for the state's preservation efforts on Jekyll Island. These tours will paint a picture of the island you've never seen before, with experienced and informative guides taking you places and showing you another side of Jekyll from their own unique perspectives.

Dolphin Tours with Captain Phillip

366 Riverview Drive, Jekyll Island, Georgia 31527
(912) 635-3152
www.captainphillip.com

Although many fishing charters double as dolphin-tour providers, there's really only one go-to dolphin charter on the island, and that's Captain Phillip's Charters and Tours.

Operating out of the Dock Office Gift Shop, which is located at the end of the Jekyll Island Club Wharf Pier, Captain Phillip specializes in dolphin tours, as well as sightseeing tours and wine tours. Tours leave out from the Jekyll Island Wharf Marina; from there, you'll spend an hour and a half aboard the Coast-Guard-certified vessel, taking in the beautiful scenery while searching for dolphins foraging in their natural habitat.

The boat has plenty of sun cover for those particularly scorching summer days, as well as a restroom to accommodate its guests. Tours run $24 per person for adults, with children three to ten boarding for $12 each. Kids two and under sail for free, with military discounts available for servicemen, women and their families.

————

Horse-drawn Carriage Tours with Three Oaks Farms
100 Stable Road, Jekyll Island, Georgia 31527
(912) 635-9500
www.threeoaksfarm.org

Three Oaks Farms offers horse-drawn carriage tours along with other equestrian services. These narrated carriage tours take participants through Jekyll's historic district, teaching riders about the historic cottages, club hotel, and more along the way. The tours are about 45 minutes long, and can be enjoyed from a traditional horse-drawn carriage seating between 4 and 15 guests, or a whimsical Cinderella carriage, which is also a popular choice for weddings and special events. They even offer evening tea tours, where guests are invited into the Jekyll Island Hotel dining room mid-tour for tea before heading back to the carriage house on Stable Road.

You can learn more about the equestrian lifestyle as well as Three Oaks Farms by checking out the section titled *Jekyll Island: An Equestrian Destination.*

————

Segway Fun Tours
100 Great Dunes Lane, Jekyll Island, Georgia 31527
(912) 635-9704

With so many history-related experiences to partake in on Jekyll, it's nice to step–or glide–into the 21st century for a welcome change of pace. Enter Jekyll Island Segway Fun Tours, Jekyll's only source for Segway rentals and guided tours.

The Segway tour introduces riders to the Segway X2 personal transportation device, known for its off-road tires enabling riders to tackle rougher terrain. These machines are revolutionary devices that do most of the balancing for riders, but getting comfortable with the Segway takes a moment to get used to. That's why Segway Fun Tours requires riders to watch a brief instructional movie before training on an obstacle course.

Navigate the obstacle course with ease and your Segway adventure awaits; flunk out and you'll be given a full refund.

Once you're comfortable riding on two wheels, you'll embark on a journey through the inland forests and trails of Jekyll's south end, learning about the indigenous flora and fauna from your tour-guide-in-tow. After you've returned from Jekyll's southern woods and pathways, you'll glide through the island's historic district, taking in the sights while wheeling your way down shell-laden streets compliments of the Segway's powerful electric motor whirling beneath your feet.

Segway Fun Tours are open most of the year, excluding January and February (the winter months are not kind to electric motors). The tours are available by reservation only, so do make time to call the number listed above. Taking a Segway tour on Jekyll Island is an experience you'll cherish for years to come.

Rates

Segway tours for 2016 run $75 per person. This includes about an hour and a half for instruction and training, with another hour and a half (three hours total) for taking a guided tour to the south end of Jekyll, then back up through the historic district before returning to base camp.

———

SSI SUP Paddleboards
1626 Frederica Road, Saint Simons Island, Georgia 31522
(912) 230-4323
ssisup.com

Jekyll Island doesn't have a retail location for paddleboards, but that won't stop the guys up at Saint Simons from bringing the paddleboard experience to you. SSI SUP stands for Saint Simons Island Stand Up Paddleboard, the go-to guides for Jekyll Island SUP.

SSI SUP offers a wide range of paddleboard services for both novice and experienced boarders alike. Meeting locations are determined during the reservation process; just let the staff know which hotel you're staying at or where you'd like to meet on Jekyll and they'll take care of the rest. Their two-hour sessions get you trained, up and on top of the paddleboard in no time, so you can spend your morning, afternoon or evening exploring Jekyll's waters from the unique perspective paddleboards provide. Paddleboard tours can take advantage of Jekyll's calm Atlantic waters, where you're guaranteed to catch some sun (and maybe a wave or two), or you can opt to meet on the riverside for a two-hour tour of Jekyll's inland waters and marshes. The stealthy progression of a self-powered paddleboard atop coastal waters makes it easier to blend in with the surrounding environment, so don't be surprised if you spot a variety of birds, bottlenose dolphins, manatees, and more on your paddleboard adventure.

While the guys and gals at SSI SUP are pretty good at getting even the shakiest of civilians upright, balanced and paddling away on one of their boards, it's not uncommon to eat water a time or two while getting the hang of SUP, so if you bring a camera or cell phone, make sure it's either waterproof or protected in a sealed waterproof pouch prior to your tour.

Because most SUP trips are contingent on current tide conditions, it's highly recommended to book your trip well in advance to ensure you get the most out of your paddle-boarding journey.

* * * * *

WILDLIFE

Jekyll Island is a lush coastal island, where the indigenous fauna has been allowed to thrive in their natural environments with minimal encroachment from humans for the last 45 years. The primary reason much of Jekyll remains unspoiled dates back to 1971, when the Georgia General Assembly passed the so-called 65/35 law, which protects a majority of the island from development to this day. The law states that no more than 35 percent of Jekyll's total land area can be used for housing, hotels, golf courses and other development, leaving 65 percent of the island in its natural, untainted state.

The law has also done wonders for the island's wildlife populations. Jekyll Island is teeming with wildlife inhabiting a wide variety of ecosystems seen on the barrier island. The Georgia Sea Turtle Center strives daily to protect Jekyll Island's healthy sea-turtle population by protecting nesting areas along Jekyll's shores, while rehabilitating injured and distressed sea turtles—along with other coastal animals—at their facility located in the historic district. 4-H Tidelands Nature Center has their finger on the pulse of Jekyll's marshlands, beaches and maritime forests, offering guided nature tours showcasing the island's flourishing plant and animal populations.

A trip to Jekyll Island would not be complete without taking advantage of the myriad opportunities to see some of Jekyll's wildlife up close and personal. Here is a brief list of what you can expect to find along Georgia's golden coast.

Sea Turtles

Many loggerhead sea turtles call Jekyll Island home during nesting season, which typically runs from March through October on the Atlantic coast (June and July are peak nesting months on Jekyll). Biologists have long used the beaches along coastal Georgia and north Florida to study the nesting behavior of sea turtles, since their short time on-shore while nesting is one of the few opportunities scientists have to observe their behavior in the wild.

Sea turtles spend most of their time underwater, crawling to shore after mating in the ocean to lay their eggs on the beach. They do this by digging out a large pit with their front flippers, and then digging out an even deeper pit with their back flippers to lay their eggs in. After the eggs have been laid, the female sea turtle takes great care to cover up and disguise the nest before slowly making her way back out into the ocean.

Sea turtle eggs take about 60 days to incubate, after which the little ones are tasked with digging out of the pit on their own, then making their way into the surf. Many of these little creatures don't make it, with dangers such as nearby predators, dehydration, and people threatening their slow journey into the sea.

Sea turtles have the world against them, with only one in every thousand estimated to survive to adulthood. That's why it's important for us to protect these endangered creatures by safeguarding our coastal shores while doing our part to make sure sea turtles can carry out their lives with as little human interaction as possible. There are several ways you can help Jekyll Island's sea turtles during your visit, should you come close to one (or many) of these majestic animals:

Don't use unapproved lights on the beach at night. Typical flashlights, lanterns, and headlights emitting artificial life can inadvertently kill baby sea turtles. That's because when sea turtles hatch, their instincts tell them to follow the brightest light, which naturally would be the light reflecting off the surface of the ocean. Baby sea turtles have been known to follow artificial lights, halting their journey to the ocean and killing many before they even get their flippers wet. Fortunately, there are sea-turtle-safe lights available that emit wavelengths deemed to be non-harmful to sea turtles, such as so-called "true red" flashlights. In fact, a local resident from across the Jekyll causeway in nearby Brunswick, Georgia has developed a turtle light that's safe for nightly beachgoers to use. Visit turtlesafeonline.com for more info.

Report sick, injured or distressed sea turtles. Sea turtles have the odds against them, and when a turtle is found hurt or injured on the beach, it's important to notify the right people. If you come across a sick, injured or otherwise distressed sea turtle, please notify the Georgia Department of Natural Resources by calling 1-800-2-SAVEME (1-800-272-8363).

Let sea turtles do their thing. Sea turtles have been around for millions of years, and have been building their nests and laying their eggs along the southern coast for just as long. They've got nesting down to a science—as long as humans don't interfere with the process. If you see a sea turtle nesting, do not approach her. If a sea turtle becomes fearful or distressed while nesting, she's likely to abort mission and head back into the ocean. Let her do her thing and this little sand-kicking miracle should go off without a hitch.

Birds

A variety of bird species can be seen scattered across and above Jekyll's beaches on a daily basis, making the island a birder's paradise. According to goldenisles.com, over 300 species of birds have been identified on the Colonial Coast Birding Trail, which runs along the Georgia coast from St. Mary's to Savannah. So if you're into birding and looking to cross a few feathered flyers off your life list, then check out some of the biggest birding stars Jekyll Island has to offer.

Ospreys – Also known as fish eagles, ospreys are all over the eastern seaboard, including the shores of Jekyll Island. These massive coastal predators have a nearly six-foot wingspan, and can often be seen during daylight hours cruising high above the beaches in search of a fresh saltwater catch.

Osprey may also be spotted hunting the grounds of Oleander at the Jekyll Island Golf Course, and are also known to reside at the Tidelands Nature Center on South Riverview Drive (Jekyll has several birding platforms constructed in an attempt to keep these massive birds from nesting on power poles).

Egrets – These stark-white herons can be seen throughout the day in Jekyll's marshes and along the Jekyll River, standing around three-feet tall and high-stepping through muddy waters in search of fish, frogs, and small insects. If you're looking to capture a memorable shot of these birds on camera, consider searching for them around Jekyll's inland marsh in the late evening just before sunset.

Wood Storks – Wood storks can be identified by their mostly white plumes outlined by dark feathers tracing their wingspan, with dark-brown heads and long, dull-colored bills. Populations are considered small on Jekyll. The wood stork has also been classified by the U.S. Fish and Wildlife Service as a threatened species, so happening across one of these on the island is a real treat. Wood storks have been spotted on several occasions in the trees surrounding the old Amphitheater pond off Stable Road, so if you make your way to these woods, keep your eyes peeled for these rare birds roosting high in the pines.

Bald Eagles – The Georgia coast has become a hot spot for bald eagle populations, with multiple nests located along the coast as well as further inland. Bald eagles were once scarce in Georgia, but have been on the rise since the passage of the Endangered Species Act in 1973. Now they can be seen in record numbers along the coast, with the Georgia Department of Natural Resources estimating around 500 eagles live in the state as of 2015.

Wilson's Plovers – These tiny coastal waders are Jekyll's migratory beach bums, sticking close to the shore in search of sandy dinners including insects, crabs and marine worms. Pointed black beaks help them locate meals in the sand, with their dark grey topcoats allowing them to blend in to their surroundings.

Sandpipers – Sandpipers are small surf feeders known for their advantageous bills that allow them to feel and detect food deep into the surf-swept sand along Jekyll's shores. One trip down to the beach is sure to produce several sandpiper sightings, with Western sandpipers making frequent appearances.

Pelicans – These large seafaring birds are all over Jekyll Island, from the eastern beaches to inland marshes. Pelicans are known for their large beaks and throat pouches that act as catch nets when scooping up fish from oceanic waters, allowing the water to escape before swallowing a meal. Gregarious in nature, don't be surprised if you spot a group of them nose-diving into fishy waters just off the coast, or posted up on one of the Jekyll River's numerous piers.

Hawks – Hawks are day-hunting birds of prey known to flourish throughout Jekyll's inland forests and fields. They are known for their incredible eyesight and keen hunting skills. When it comes to their diet, hawks prefer a variety of meals from mice and moles to chipmunks, squirrels–even other birds. Hawks can be found on Jekyll by looking for places they would hunt, such as open fields and tall grassy areas.

Seagulls – When it comes to seagulls, you should always remember one rule: if you feed a gull once, then be prepared to feed a thousand of his friends. Seagulls can easily be identified by their greyish-white plumes, combined with a hideous squawk used to signal others that someone's got food. Seagulls should have to work for their food. Please do not feed the gulls.

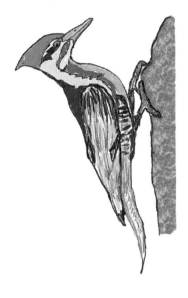

Woodpeckers – if you hear a distinct knocking sound coming from the nearby trees on the island, don't be surprised if you look up to find one of Jekyll's many woodpeckers foraging for food throughout the forest canopy. Several species of woodpeckers can be seen across Jekyll Island, but your chances of spotting one increase significantly when you stick to the maritime forests on the northernmost and southernmost portions of the island.

Birds that are both permanent residents as well as migratory visitors to Jekyll Island can be found all across this barrier island, but there are a few specific locations you should check out with binoculars in hand. The Jekyll Island Information Center has an observation deck right behind the center and overlooking the marshes. St. Andrews Picnic Area on Jekyll's south end has an observation deck as well that overlooks Jekyll Sound. Several bird nesting areas exist in the dunes surrounding Glory Beach, and a birding trail puts north-end explorers on a variety of coastal birds inhabiting the Driftwood Beach/Clam Creek area.

Want to learn more about the world of birding on Jekyll Island?
Georgiawildlife.org has a great "Birds of Georgia's Colonial Coast Birding Trail" checklist available for both serious birders and recreational birdwatchers alike. Also be sure to check out Tidelands Nature Center, the official "birding hot spot" of Jekyll Island.

Alligators

If you were wondering whether or not coastal Georgia was far enough south to comfortably house a few indigenous alligators, well wonder no more. American alligators are permanent fixtures on Jekyll Island, thriving particularly around the island's interior freshwater ponds. The alligators of Jekyll have done a fine job assimilating with their semi-developed surroundings, and can be seen regularly in the water hazards of Jekyll Island Golf Course, as well as the old duck pond on the Crane Road Bike Trail between Ben Fortson Parkway and Stable Road.

Unlike their crocodile cousins, alligators don't possess the ability to secrete salt efficiently, so their time spent is saltwater must remain limited. That's precisely why you're more likely to run into an alligator basking in the sun or trolling through the freshwaters of the island interior. Alligators are also ectothermic reptiles, meaning they rely on the surrounding environment to regulate body temperature.

You're more likely to encounter an alligator doing absolutely nothing as opposed to spotting one on the run, but don't let their apparent lethargy fool you: these creatures can move fast when they want to. If you see an alligator in the wild, keep a safe distance between you and the reptile. And if you lose a golf ball near the water, just take a drop and play through, because fishing around in Jekyll's numerous inland ponds is a good way to end up with a wooden hand.

Snakes

Talking about snakes in the South could provoke a slap from an older local within earshot, considering antiquated superstitions imply such cold-blooded creatures can be "talked up" or summoned by the mere mention of their name. Here we'd like to take a moment to expel such notions, and instead shed some light on why these reptilian residents of Jekyll Island are so important to the local ecosystem.

Jekyll Island lies in a geographical region of the world flourishing with an abundance of subtropical life. The temperate year-round climate makes the barrier island a hospitable environment for an abundance of life, including snakes. According to the Applied Wildlife Conservation Lab at the Jekyll Island Georgia Sea Turtle Center, there are currently 12 species of non-venomous snakes residing on Jekyll, and three species of venomous snakes totaling 15 species in all.

These 15 species of snakes are able to thrive on an island a mere seven miles long and a mile or so wide, because they are not directly competing with scarce food sources for sustenance. What does that mean, exactly? It means creatures such as mice, rats, toads, lizards, cockroaches, and other small pests and prey find the habitat just as hospitable, and would overrun the island if not for the wide variety of predatory snakes maintaining the balance on Jekyll.

While running across a snake on Jekyll Island might cause quite a fright, as long as you keep a safe distance and do not provoke them, there's usually nothing to worry about. Although every snake should be treated as a poisonous one for safety purposes, it is worthwhile to become familiar with the island's three venomous snakes:

Eastern Diamondback Rattlesnakes – Of all the species of rattlesnakes currently recognized, these formidable island inhabitants are the largest, ranging from three to six-feet long, with fully-grown specimens weighing nearly ten pounds. Identifying these snakes is simple: a distinct pattern of brown or tan diamonds lines the back of these rattlesnakes from head to tail, outlined by lighter-colored scales highlighting their title. Rattlesnakes also have distinctive heads, broad and triangular in shape, and much wider than the rest of their bodies.

Timber Rattlesnakes – Aside from the trademark triangular head associated with every species of rattlesnake, timber rattlesnakes, also known as canebrake snakes, are camouflaged rather differently from their diamondback cousins, making them more efficient hunters in environments such as cane thickets and high brush, thus attributing to their name. The patterns on their back trade diamonds for chevrons, which are distinctive "V" shapes that point upward toward the head. Timber rattlers are also lighter in color, yet have solid black tails, with dark scales extended just above the rattler.

Cottonmouth snakes – Cottonmouth snakes get their name from their distinctive white-pinkish mouths. These snakes are also known as water moccasins throughout the South, and can come in a variety of colors. Younger cottonmouths usually don the brightest colors, with bright tan and medium-brown stripes, whereas older cottonmouths sport darker scales, and can appear almost black in some cases. Cottonmouths are also rather thick, heavy snakes, averaging around two to four feet in length.

The state of Georgia protects its non-venomous snakes by deeming it illegal to kill one, however, it is not illegal to kill a venomous snake in Georgia because of their status as a potential danger or nuisance to individuals coming in contact with them.

This does not mean it is acceptable to kill a venomous snake of Jekyll Island. Both venomous and non-venomous snakes play an important role in keeping other nuisance animals such as rats and mice to a minimum. In an effort to better protect both people and reptilian wildlife of Jekyll Island, the Applied Wildlife Conservation Lab has actually instituted a radio telemetry program aimed at tracking and studying indigenous eastern-diamondback populations. This study, implemented in

2011, has divulged a plethora of data on diamondback populations, behaviors, and responses to urban development, as well as assessing wildlife management alternatives to further protect both snakes and humans.

What if a snake bites me?

Snakes are everywhere throughout the South, whether you know it or not. Unless you directly squash the tail of a snake with a size-11 steel-toed boot, odds are they'll leave you alone. Don't mess with snakes, and usually they won't mess with you. Still, snakebites do occur, so if you happen to find yourself sporting a fresh snakebite, **don't panic**. Instead, focus on what you need to do next:

Dial 911 – This should be a reflex, and no matter what, is the very first step you need to take.

Remain calm and restrict movement – Panicking will get your blood flowing faster, moving the poison through your bloodstream at an accelerated rate. So will moving around a lot, so if possible, keep still until emergency crews arrive. If you're in Jekyll backcountry and have to get to the nearest road or identifying landmark to meet emergency workers, keep your heart elevated above the snakebite wound as you move, e.g. if a snake bit your hand, keep it as low as possible and to your side.

Do NOT use a tourniquet – Snake venom is super-toxic in concentrated form, with toxicity to cells reduced as the venom becomes more and more diluted. That means venom that is already inside you is diluted within your own blood stream—even more so if you're fully hydrated. Placing a tourniquet near a wound will just cause a rush of concentrated venom to be released once it's removed, causing extreme damage to nearby cells.

Do NOT try to suck out the poison – This old Wild-West myth is simply ineffective, and can cause further damage to nearby cells by increasing the risk of infection. Cutting a bite wound is even worse, so don't even think about it. Just concentrate on seeking medical attention as soon as possible.

Positive identification of the snake – If you've killed the snake, maintain the utmost caution while bringing in the dead snake for positive identification. Snakeheads can reflexively bite for up to three days after they've been killed, so be careful. Do not try to hunt the snake if it got away—you'd just be wasting your time. If the snake flees, continue to recall any distinctive patterns and/or head shape, burning it into your mind as you make your way to (or wait for) emergency medical professionals.

For more information on snakebite first aid, check out the Mayo Clinic's advice by visiting mayoclinic.org.

If you have any questions about snake research and conservation efforts taking place on Jekyll Island, check out the Applied Wildlife Conservation Lab webpage by visiting wildlifelab.wix.com/jekyllresearch.

Dolphins

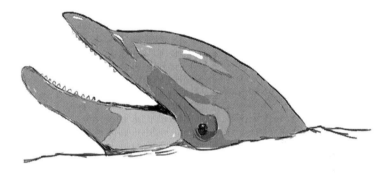

The myriad waters of Jekyll Island are home to some of the coolest mammals to thrive in the Atlantic Ocean: the bottlenose dolphin. These highly intelligent sea mammals have a long, storied history with human interactions, from military-trained dolphins locating underwater hazards and enemy combatants, to dolphins learning a number of commands, performing in live shows, and exhibiting a level of brainpower unrivaled by any other ocean-dweller creature. The brain-to-body ratio of a dolphin's gray matter is actually second only to humans, which likely explains their impressive intellect, along with their ability to communicate and solve problems.

Bottlenose dolphins travel in pods, meaning groups of dolphins consisting of anywhere from a dozen to three-dozen individuals. They are often seen in groups trolling off Jekyll's Atlantic shores just past the sandbar and breakers, as well as on the inland side in the Jekyll River and surrounding marshes. It's not uncommon to spot dolphin fins from the road the moment you hit the Jekyll Island causeway, considering they spend a lot of time foraging for meals in the brackish waters surrounding Jointer Island (the moment you turn on the Jekyll Island causeway, Jointer Island is the small land mass to your right).

Dolphins can also be spotted in the murky waters of the Jekyll River hunting fish using the power of sound. Dolphins don't rely solely on sight to locate fish; instead, they use echolocation to determine where their next meal is coming from. Echolocation works like sonar: the dolphin emits a sound, then listens for the echo to determine how far away a potential meal is. Dolphins also use a variety of sounds to communicate with one another, making these incredibly vocal mammals the chattiest creatures you'd ever encounter under the sea.

To book a dolphin tour on Jekyll Island, consider giving Captain Phillips a call at (912) 635-3152.

* * * * *

RULES OF THE ISLAND

Jekyll Island isn't synonymous with a Miami Beach free-for-all. In fact, if you're looking for a place to visit with all of your twenty-something club-hopping buddies while floating your livers for a solid week, then you may want to reconsider your travel plans. Both the state of Georgia and Jekyll's residents have long fought to keep the island a quiet, peaceful, and family friendly destination.

That doesn't mean you can't have fun on the island, but there are some no-nonsense rules in place to protect not only residents and visitors, but the indigenous wildlife and fragile ecosystems as well. Several regulations exist that may seem a little extreme–like having ordinary flashlights on the beach at night–but there are good reasons for every statute in place, so please take a moment to check out some of the rules and ordinances that currently apply anyone visiting Jekyll Island.

Important Information for Pet Owners

Jekyll Island loves your pets (almost) as much as you do. If you're looking for a vacation destination that is pet-friendly and accommodating, then you've found the right shoreline for your next trip with your four-legged friend(s).

Jekyll's beaches are a paradise for dogs and their owners, giving K9s plenty of space to run free along the shore while experiencing the joy of having a little sand between their paws. Take a stroll down to Jekyll's beaches on any given day and you're sure to see dogs and their owners playing with Frisbees, tennis balls, and rope toys while taking in the ocean view.

Jekyll Island is a great place to create some memories with your canine companion, as long as you adhere to a few simple rules for bringing your furry friends along with you on your trip. The current pet regulations for Jekyll Island are as follows:

Dogs must be kept under the control of their owners. While dogs are officially required to remain on a leash no longer than 16 feet, this isn't strictly enforced as long as pet owners are behaving responsibly with their dogs. Jekyll's beaches offer plenty of space to run–especially during low tide–so consider your surroundings when you're perusing the beaches with your pet. If you're on a crowded section of beach, be considerate of other beachgoers in your vicinity while keeping your pet(s) close by.

Absolutely NO PETS on the south end of Jekyll Island. Most of Jekyll's beaches are fair game for pet owners, with one exception: the island's south end between South Dunes Picnic Area and 2000' northeast of Saint Andrews Picnic Area. The reason for the restriction isn't arbitrary, and has been put in place to protect the wildlife that often calls the south end of the island home. Migratory birds, for example, often nest off the shores of Jekyll's south end. Any pet owner can easily imagine how their dog might react to a flock of birds trying to nest within eyesight–disrupting such a scene would be irresistible to any red-blooded canine. So for the sake of our feathered friends, this is the only section of beach where pets are strictly prohibited.

Pet owners must remove and dispose of all fecal matter. This one seems like a no-brainer and should go without saying, but we're saying it anyway: pick up after your pet. It's considerate, sanitary, and will allow others to get the same enjoyment out of their Jekyll beach experience as you've had. Because no one else wants to stumble upon your pet's poop.

Speed Limits

Jekyll Island is a pedestrian's paradise for several reasons, one being the strictly enforced speed limits across the island. Don't be surprised if you see Georgia State Patrol cars on several occasions throughout your stay; these guys and gals absolutely will not hesitate to write you a ticket should you be caught breaking the speed limit during your trip.

While Jekyll's speed limits may seem a little frustrating, most people understand that they are necessary to keep the island operating at a peaceful, island pace. So be sure to adhere to all posted speed limits, and avoid pulling the old "10 over is okay" trick, because it won't work here. Besides, you're on an island, and you really shouldn't be in a hurry anyway.

The island-wide speed limit on Jekyll is 35 miles per hour, unless otherwise posted. The central portion of the island, including the historic district, the new beach village area, and side streets have even slower limits posted, so be aware of the slow automobile speed requirements when cruising through Jekyll's busy areas.

Beach Rules

Like we said before, this isn't Cancun, and the beach isn't a free-for-all. Jekyll Island is a very family friendly place to visit, with beach rules and regulations that were put in place to adhere to Jekyll's consideration for the creatures and kiddos roaming the shores.

Stay off the sand dunes. Thanks to the Jekyll Island Authority's tedious conservation efforts, the sand dunes on the island are quite abundant. While Jekyll's dunes make beautiful backdrops for any beach vacation, their purpose extends far beyond their appearances. Sand dunes are natural buffers that separate developments and inland structures from the hazardous conditions like strong tides, massive waves and heavy winds that oceans deliver. Therefore, walking on or across the sand dunes on Jekyll Island is strictly prohibited. There are plenty of crossovers and boardwalks to get you from inland terrain to the beaches, so please use them accordingly.

Do not approach marked turtle nests. Jekyll Island is known for its large sea turtle population, cared for and watched over by the Jekyll Island Sea Turtle Center. Center employees remind beachgoers to stay away from marked turtle nests at all times. The less we mess with these amazing ocean-dwelling creatures, the longer they'll be around for our enjoyment.

Swim at your own risk. While Jekyll strives to maintain a safe beach atmosphere for families, it is beyond their capacity to monitor every stretch of beach at every waking moment. That's why swimming on Jekyll Island means swimming at your own risk.

No driving on the beach. This isn't Daytona, and venturing onto Jekyll's sandy beaches could land you in hot water, so make sure to keep your tires on the pavement.

No glass containers on the beach. If you're going to bring a cooler full of beverages down to the water, you'll have to leave the bottles at home. Make sure the drinks you carry with you to the beach are in aluminum or plastic containers.

No beach bonfires allowed. If you were thinking of roasting marshmallows while listening to the waves crash, then you'll have to think again. No fires are allowed on Jekyll's beaches, and for good reason. Apart from the risk of starting a wildfire in nearby maritime forests, the light from beach fires could potentially harm and confuse sea turtle hatchlings that are trying to make their way into the ocean.

Metal detectors are not allowed. Save your treasure hunting for another time and place, because a Jekyll Island ordinance bans the use of electronic devices for mineral, metal, and artifact detection. That doesn't mean you can't use your trusty plastic shovel to dig around the beaches in search of booty, just make sure you turn over anything you find to the nearest pirates or swashbucklers.

No fireworks allowed. Although Georgia did finally catch up with its neighboring states by legalizing fireworks effective July 1st, 2015, they're still prohibited from use on Jekyll's beaches. That may seem like a bummer at first glance, but discharging fireworks on Jekyll Island would pose several hazards to the fragile ecosystems that span the island, so just don't do it.

Other Rules of the Island

No overnight parking in public areas. Like we've said before, the Georgia State Patrol does an incredible job ensuring rules are followed on Jekyll, and that goes for leaving automobiles in public parking lots as well.

If you park overnight in a public lot, you risk your vehicle being towed, so just don't do it.

Do not feed the wildlife. Feeding wild animals on Jekyll Island is strictly prohibited.

No freshwater fishing on Jekyll Island. The saltwater fishing off Jekyll's beaches and the Intracoastal Waterway is always welcomed, however, freshwater fishing on Jekyll is not allowed. There are several ponds and lakes scattered throughout the inland terrain of Jekyll, so if you happen upon one, don't be tempted. Besides, the fish are much, much bigger in the ocean.

* * * * *

JEKYLL ISLAND BEACHES

It's where the surf meets the sand, and it may just be your main reason for heading to Jekyll for your vacation getaway. We can't blame you, because the beaches of Jekyll Island are no doubt one of the most attractive features the island has to offer.

Jekyll's beaches are unique in several ways. The sand is as natural as it gets–nothing on Jekyll's shores is trucked in, with the exception of tourists. The water stays relatively warm throughout the year, especially close to the beaches, where the island's undersea geography provides shallow waters miles from the shore compared to beaches that drop off suddenly once off the coast. Jekyll's waters are often as calm as a lake, making it a great location for standup paddleboards, calm-water waders, saltwater fisherman and beach bums on pool floats. Of course, things tend to pick up a bit when storms roll through.

Jekyll has three main beaches, each with their own reasons for visiting. If you're camping on the north end, then it's hard to miss Driftwood Beach, a must-see for its arborous seaside embellishments. If you're riding bikes on the south end, then you're likely to happen upon Glory Beach, the site of several scenes from 1989's major motion picture *Glory*. And finally, no one can miss the main beach at Great Dunes, the longest, easternmost stretch of beach lining Jekyll Island.

Great Dunes

The first glimpse you get of the Atlantic Ocean on your trip to Jekyll Island will most likely come across the sands of Great Dunes Beach, located on the easternmost side of Jekyll Island. Great Dunes Beach stretches across almost four miles of coastline, spanning from South Dunes Park on the southern end to Driftwood Beach on the north.

Great Dunes Park borders Great Dunes Beach, and provides visitors with several amenities to make their visit as pleasurable as possible. Located off North Beachview Drive, just a few yards north of the Jekyll Island Conference Center, Great Dunes Park has grassy areas for picnics, covered awnings and tables for those looking to eat in the shade, grills, bathrooms, water fountains, boardwalk showerheads, park benches, and paved paths meandering alongside Jekyll's great easterly dunes.

Great Dunes Park also has a large covered pavilion for large groups, plenty of parking spaces in a central island location, and is a great jumping off point for island adventures like hitting Jekyll's coastal bike trails or catching a round of mini-golf across the street. If you're looking for a central location to set up shop for your day near Jekyll's beaches, think Great Dunes Park.

———

Driftwood Beach

On the northern end of Jekyll Island, secluded from the hustle and bustle of the historic district and hotel traffic, you'll find a tranquil shoreline where weathered natural beauty is on full display. That shore is called Driftwood Beach.

Driftwood Beach is a must-see for every visitor to Jekyll Island. Named for the countless expired trees scattering up the coast and creating a labyrinth during high tide for beach explorers to navigate through, Driftwood Beach offers a thousand photo opportunities and memorable vistas, all rolled up into one location off Jekyll's beaten path.

The driftwood environment is the result of Jekyll's northernmost shore being slowly eroded away. The shoreline we can see today would most likely be completely gone if Jekyll were affected by non-stop waves, but the fact that Jekyll is situated in shallow waters and far from the Atlantic's continental shelf means waves are long gone by the time they even get close to Jekyll's beaches. This results in slowly formed tidal coastlines–during a typical weather season.

One exception to the theory of slow erosion took place in the late summer of 1964, when Hurricane Dora plowed through coastal towns from North Florida to the Golden Isles. Damage was estimated to top $1 million dollars on Jekyll alone, with devastated shorelines prompting President Johnson to have boulders trucked in to protect Georgia's Gem from storm-driven erosion in the future. Locals that can still recall the last major hurricane to hit the island eponymously call these rocks "Johnson Rocks". You can still see these boulders forming a line and protecting the driftwood trees along this northern stretch of beach.

If you're heading to Driftwood Beach, don't forget to bring:

Your camera gear – Driftwood Beach is one of the best places on the entire island for pictures. Don't be surprised if you see other families getting family portraits made. It's also fun to get couples and group photos with St. Simons Lighthouse in the background, so if you've got a long lens, make sure to bring it with you.

Flip flops – Walking along Driftwood Beach makes for a comfortable stroll, but getting there after parking several hundred feet away can be hard on your soles. You don't want to get sand in your shoes, either, so make sure to bring the flip flops or beach sandals along for your trip.

Your morning coffee – Driftwood Beach makes for a great trip any time of day, but in the morning the beach is simply phenomenal. That's because sunrise on Driftwood Beach paints the Atlantic and the beach's wooden residents with colors and hues that would make any artist's mouth water. If you're looking for an unforgettable sunrise, be sure to make Driftwood Beach one of your morning stops during your stay on Jekyll Island.

———

Glory Beach

Glory Beach is situated between South Dunes Beach and Saint Andrews Beach on the southeastern stretch of the island. Several battle scenes from the 1989 civil war epic *Glory* were filmed on this isolated stretch of the island. According to the website www.movie-locations.com, the beach was utilized for scenes portraying the nighttime assault on Fort Wagner, as well as the tragic aftermath.

The best part about Glory Beach is its relative isolation from more popular areas of the island. It's not uncommon to spend an afternoon strolling down Glory Beach without seeing a single set of footprints other than your own. Views of Little Cumberland Island can be seen from the beach by looking southward across the inlet.

Getting to Glory Beach can be confusing for out-of-towners, considering you won't find a huge sign advertising the beach. Instead, look for the entrance to the Jekyll Island Soccer Complex by heading south on South Beachview Drive, a little over two miles from the roundabout at Ben Fortson Parkway. There is a sign at the entrance of the Jekyll Island Soccer Complex on your left (if you pass the Jekyll Island 4-H Center on your left then you've gone too far).

Parking in the gravel soccer complex parking lot will give you access to Glory Beach via the Glory Beach boardwalk. The boardwalk, spanning just over 200 yards, will take you on a long walk across protected nesting areas and dunes all the way to one of Jekyll's most unscathed shorelines.

***

Other Parking/Beach Access Points

Water Tank Beach Path

Just 0.55 miles south of the Hampton Inn & Suites off South Beachview Drive lies a short beach access trail that is sure to get you away from the

summer crowds packing the beaches on the north end. If you're southbound on South Beachview Drive and past the Hampton, you can't miss the water tank on your right. Parking for beach access is directly across from the tank on your left–just make sure you don't block the gate (your vehicle will be towed at your expense).

Saint Andrews Picnic Area

There's plenty of parking at the Saint Andrews Picnic Area, as well as easy beach access to Jekyll's shores on the south end. Less than a hundred yards lies between the parking lot and the beach, making Saint Andrews a great beach alternative for individuals that may have trouble walking long distances to get to the water.

There's also a handicap-accessible ramp on Saint Andrews for wheelchairs and walkers that leads down to the water, as well as restrooms and water fountains on the east end of the parking area.

The Beach Pavilion off North Beachview Drive

Just a quarter mile north of Great Dunes and Tortuga Jacks lies The Beach Pavilion, on the right side of the road on North Beachview Drive. Plenty of parking, restrooms, and covered seating overlooking the Atlantic make the pavilion an excellent home base for a day on the beach.

***

Knowing Your Beach Flags

Beach flags are important indicators of current water conditions, and should be the first thing you check for before heading into the surf. There are five different flags to indicate varying degrees of danger and/or awareness, so make sure you know what each one means prior to your trip.

Double Red Flag – This flag means the water is closed to the public. When a double-red flag is flying, avoiding the water isn't a suggestion, and beachgoers entering the water could face fines.

Single Red Flag – The single red flag indicates a high hazard due to strong currents and high surf. It is advised never to enter the water on a red-flag day, regardless of whether one or two red flags are flying.

Yellow Flag – The yellow flag is like the yellow light at a traffic signal, and essentially means the same thing: caution. Yellow flags are raised when moderate surf conditions are observed.

Green Flag – Green flag means go! Conditions are calm and the waters are welcoming, with the green flag giving water babies the go-ahead to get out there and have a good time.

Purple Flag – The purple flag means dangerous marine life has been spotted in the area, so beachgoers are advised to exercise caution when dipping their toes in the surf. The purple flag could indicate anything from pesky jellyfish to a shark sighting, so swim at your own risk.

* * * * *

NORTH END

Clam Creek Picnic Area
10 Clam Creek Road, Jekyll Island, Georgia 31527

Situating on the island's northernmost end where North Beachview and Riverview Roads collide is Clam Creek Picnic Area, directly across the street from the Jekyll Island Campground. Named for the saltmarsh creek running alongside the eastside of the road leading into the picnic pavilions and parking area, Clam Creek Picnic Area is a must-visit for every active outdoor enthusiast.

Several activities can be kicked off at Clam Creek. For starters, there's the creek itself, known to be a favorite fishing spot for locals and tourists alike. There's also a huge covered fishing pier lying at the north end of Clam Creek Picnic Area, giving anglers easy access to the waters of the Jekyll

River, as well as the Jekyll Island Fishing Center: your one-stop shop for bait, tackle, refreshments and more.

For horse lovers, Clam Creek Picnic Area is also a jumping-off point for Three Oaks Farms horseback riding tours along the northern beaches and through the maritime forests of Jekyll Island. Several horseback-riding trails exist on this northern stretch of the island, taking riders through several different ecosystems from the outer coastline to the inland canopies.

Of course, hooves aren't required when exploring Clam Creek, and there are plenty of paved trails to accommodate runners, joggers and strollers seeking a quiet, unspoiled location to get their daily cardio in. While Clam Creek Picnic Area does tend to get busy in spurts (primarily from anglers around the fishing pier, bridge and creekside), there are plenty of opportunities to get away from the crowds.

One trail in particular that is usually secluded is the northern Clam Creek Bike Trail. This trail runs 1.3 miles from the trailhead at the Clam Creek Picnic Area to the intersection of the north Driftwood Beach access point (2.6 miles round trip). The asphalt trail is perfect for runners seeking a place that's easy on the feet with astonishing scenery to boot.

There are also grills, picnic tables, and plenty of shade available at Clam Creek Picnic Area. Astounding views of Brunswick's Sydney Lanier Bridge lie to the west of Clam Creek, and don't be surprised if you spot a massive car carrier, barge or The Emerald Princess Casino sailing through the Intracoastal Waterway, into Saint Simons Sound and east toward the Atlantic.

Consider a visit by taking either Riverview Drive to Clam Creek Road, or North Beachview Drive to Clam Creek Road, right in front of the Jekyll Island Campground.

———

Jekyll Island Campground
1197 Riverview Drive, Jekyll Island, Georgia 31527
(912) 635-3021
www.jekyllisland.com/campground

Speaking of Clam Creek, it's hard to miss the Jekyll Island Campground directly across the street from Clam Creek Road on Jekyll's secluded north end. The Jekyll Island Campground caters to traditional campers with tents in hand, as well as RV campers seeking reliable hookups with all the bells and whistles one would expect in the modern world.

Campers can expect to find primitive tent sites, water and electric sites, as well as full hookups to accommodate campers in tow. Over 200 campsites exist in the campground's 18+ acres of subtropical forest. Campsites are spacious with plenty of shade, and are located in a section of Jekyll known for its serenity on Jekyll's north end. Each campsite also comes with a picnic table and a fire pit, two must-haves for any serious camper.

There is also a general store serving as the campground headquarters located at the entrance to the grounds. There you'll find all the camping extras you'd ever need (and may have left at home), from firewood and matches to snack items and soft drinks. They also have propane pumping directly across from the campground store, with laundry, showers, computer port, recycling and trash down the main drag just a few yards up from the general store on the right.

You can find more information about the campground, as well as view a detailed campground map, by visiting jekyllisland.com/campground.

———

Horton House Ruins

The Jekyll Island Historic District may represent a vibrant past during the island's so-called Gilded Age of the early 20th century, but the historical beginning of English influence on the island lies just to the north off Riverview Drive at the historic Horton House.

The Horton House that stands today was constructed in 1743, making the remaining edifice one of Georgia's oldest standing tabby structures, and one of Jekyll Island's most cherished buildings. Spanish soldiers, following their unsuccessful raid on Saint Simon's Fort Frederica in July of 1742, destroyed the original Horton House during their retreat back to Saint Augustine.

The house as we know it today was named for Major William Horton, an Englishman who served in James Oglethorpe's regiment chartered by the British to colonize coastal Georgia in 1732. Horton's arrival in Georgia marked the first time an Englishman would call Jekyll Island his home.

Although the Jekyll Island of the mid-18th century held strategic importance for the British in their battle to ward off the Spanish to the south, most of the major action along the Georgia/Florida coast took place to the north at Fort Frederica on Saint Simons Island, and as far south as the Spanish-occupied Castillo de San Marcos in Saint Augustine, Florida.

Horton took advantage of the peace that followed the Spanish withdrawal from coastal Georgia in 1742 by establishing a flourishing homestead, complete with crops used for personal sustenance as well as exporting foodstuffs to the habitants of Saint Simons Island. Horton also had a brewery on the island, making the Horton batch Georgia's first known beer.

Horton passed away in Savannah in 1748, and during the late 18th century ownership of the island fell into the hands of the DuBignon family. The DuBignons took up residence at Horton House after making several repairs and additions. Now the Horton House stands as a relic of the very first English influence to fall upon Jekyll Island's unspoiled land.

———

DuBignon Cemetery

Directly across Riverview Drive from the Horton House on the marsh side lies the DuBignon cemetery. Gravestones marking Jekyll's first full-time French residents reside within the cemetery walls, even though there are some doubts as to the true final resting place of the DuBignon clan.

It is thought by many locals that unmarked DuBignon graves are scattered throughout the cemetery area on the marsh side of the property. Christophe Anne Poulain DuBignon, a French naval captain and owner of both Sapelo Island and Jekyll Island, was buried underneath a live oak tree close to DuBignon Creek. The exact location of the grave is unknown to this day.

For just under a century, the DuBignons reigned on Jekyll, from the acquisition of the island in 1794 to the Jekyll Island Club's purchase of the island in 1886. In fact, the grave of the man who actually sold the island to the club, John Eugene DuBignon, is among the others at the marsh-side cemetery. These graves, along with the Horton House itself, remain the few Jekyll Island relics left from a revolutionary time period marking the establishment of English colonization on the Georgia coast.

* * * * *

SOUTH END

Jekyll Island 4-H Center
550 South Beachview Drive, Jekyll Island, Georgia 31527
Main Office: (912) 635-4115
Environmental Education Office: (912) 635-4117
4-H Center Director: Donna Stewart
www.jekyll4h.org

If you're a member of the millennial generation who happened to grow up in the Peach State, then there's a good chance you ventured to Jekyll Island's 4-H Center as a kid.

According to www.jekyll4h.org, 13,000 people a year have made their way through Jekyll's 4-H Center since 1983, with 2014 becoming the year marking their 1 millionth visitor to the facility. The center is surrounded by nature trails and coastal workshops meant to teach children everything there is to know about Georgia's coastal environment.

A lot has been going on at the Jekyll Island 4-H Center in recent years, with construction of a new facility underway through 2016. If you would like more information about future camps and programs offered at the 4-H Center, please contact the center at the numbers listed above.

_____

4-H Tidelands Nature Center
100 South Riverview Drive, Jekyll Island, Georgia 31527
(912) 635-5032
www.tidelands4h.org

4-H Tidelands Nature Center is where learning about Georgia's coastal environment means getting your hands dirty. Tidelands Nature Center offers several hands-on activities for groups affiliated with schools and educational programs, as well as the general public.

Live animal exhibits give visitors access to coastal creatures such as sea turtles, snakes, alligators and a variety of crustaceans, while guided nature trail tours take explorers through three diverse habitats of Georgia's coastal environment. You'll traverse along Jekyll's beaches, the interior island maritime forests, and the westward salt marshes buffering Jekyll from the Intracoastal Waterway and the mainland.

Kayaking, canoeing, and paddle boating are also activities offered at Tidelands. Call ahead to see about group discounts and seasonal specials before stopping by.

_____

Summer Waves Water Park
210 South Riverview Drive, Jekyll Island, Georgia 31527
(912) 635-2074

Just south of the 4-H Tidelands Nature Center on South Riverview Drive is an attraction that's hard to miss: Summer Waves Water Park. With water slides for thrill seekers, a lazy river for cautious compadres, and a wave pool for those somewhere in between, Summer Waves is worth every penny during Jekyll's hot and humid summer months.

Are you traveling to Jekyll outside of peak-heat months and unsure about hitting up a water park? Consider this: according to Intellicast Weather, the average temps for May don't reach below 67 degrees, with the average high at 82. June, July, and August are obvious safe bets with average highs reaching low high 80s to low 90s, with September's high reaching 85 and October's at 78.

Our recommendation? Middle of May through the month of September and you'll be sure to have plenty of high-humidity reasons to visit the park. In fact, our recommendation based on average temps coincides with the Summer Waves 2015 schedule (the park opened mid-May and was only open on weekends mid-August through September). Tickets start at $19.95 per adult via jekyllisland.com, with kids under 48" getting in at the junior rate of $15.95. Discounts apply for large groups, seniors, and kids 3 and under, with rates and hours subject to change, so make sure to call ahead before planning your trip.

St. Andrews Picnic Area

Located on the southern tip of Jekyll Island where South Beachview Drive and South Riverview Drive collide, St. Andrews Picnic Area offers panoramic views across Jekyll Sound toward Brunswick and abroad from a convenient location that's easy to get to via bike, vehicle, or on foot.

This portion of the island receives minimal traffic year-round, with tourists spending most of their time at either the central portion of the island surrounding Jekyll Island Historic District or at the beaches on the island's eastern seaboard.

Much of St. Andrews picnic area is shaded, making it perfect for picnics under a canopy of Spanish moss and live oak trees. The picnic area also provides plenty of parking, as well as restrooms, picnic tables, and a two-story observation deck at the end of one of Jekyll's well-maintained trails.

Saint Andrews is also known for its easy access to the beach. Parking on the west end of the parking lot gets visitors within a hundred yards of the water. There's also a handicap-accessible ramp on Saint Andrews to help folks down to the shoreline from the picnic area.

Photo opportunities abound at South Jekyll, where vistas of Cumberland Island toward the Atlantic side put Georgia's Golden Isles in perspective. To the west of the observation deck flow the waters of Jekyll Sound, fed by three rivers; The Satilla, Little Satilla, and Brunswick River.

The dunes and beach area are well maintained by the Jekyll Island Authority, resulting in a clean, natural setting for families to enjoy. So if you're looking for a peaceful place on the island to spend time with family and friends, St. Andrews Picnic Area is a great place to start.

––––––––

South Dunes Picnic Area

100 yards south of the Hampton Inn Suites on South Beachview Drive lies the South Dunes Picnic Area. Shaded by live oak trees and sheltered from coastal winds by high dunes separating the area from the beaches, South Dunes Picnic Area is a unique place to hold a family gathering, outdoor event, or of course, have a picnic.

South Dunes is accommodated with grills for cooking out, screened pavilions for especially buggy days, paved walking trails and beach access via the boardwalks rising above the high dunes toward the back of the park. There is plenty of parking and plenty of shade making it an excellent location to take a sack lunch on a scorching summer day.

If you decide to get your walk in while at South Dunes, be on the lookout for local wildlife. Although we've never seen any alligators in the pond located within the picnic area, there are plenty of signs warning visitors to remain cautious when strolling close to the water's edge, so just keep that in mind when you're scouting out the area. If you see something in the water that looks kind of like an alligator's eyes and snout just breaking the water's surface, then it probably is.

HISTORIC DISTRICT

Listed as a National Historic Landmark District since 1978, the Jekyll Island Historic District gives visitors a glimpse into the Gilded Age of Jekyll's past. There are thirty-three buildings that make up the historic district, from a small boiler-house-turned-ice-cream shop, to the massive complex making up the Jekyll Island Club Hotel and adjoining Annex. Strolling these historic streets is sure to take you back to a time of decadence and leisure, while evoking a poignant reminder that even for the wealthiest of individuals, nothing lasts forever.

Georgia Sea Turtle Center
214 Stable Road, Jekyll Island, Georgia 31527
(912) 635-4444
gstc.jekyllisland.com

The Georgia Sea Turtle Center, located at the heart of Jekyll Island just off Hopkins Road, is the only institution offering sea turtle rehabilitation in the state of Georgia. The center has several roles catering to both sea turtles and the general public. On the sea-turtle side, the facility is a fully functional hospital for injured and distressed sea turtles that need medical attention.

For upright tourists, the center was also designed to raise awareness for sea turtle conservation to the general public through interactive galleries and viewing areas. Loads of information about Georgia's sea turtle population is available through the center, from how they've evolved through the millennia, to how their populations have been impacted by pollution, irresponsible fishing practices, and coastal development.

The main touring area also features a window into the hospital portion of the center, where biologists actually work with sea turtle patients to get them the treatment they need before introducing them back into the wild. Many of the center's hard-shelled patients include sea turtles that have been captured in fishing nets, caught in offshore traps, and found by beachcombers in a distressed state and in serious need of medical attention.

The facility is open year-round, with rates currently at $7 for adults and $5 for kids 4-12 years old. Kids 3 and under currently get into the center for free. Both Living Social as well as Groupon regularly offer discounted rates for entrance into the center, so they're worth checking out before purchasing tickets onsite.

___

Jekyll Island Club Hotel
371 Riverview Drive, Jekyll Island, Georgia 31527
(855) 219-7338
www.jekyllclub.com

For almost 130 years, the cylindrical turret rising above the Jekyll Island Club Hotel has been the beacon marking the epicenter of Jekyll Island's Historic District. Morgans, Rockefellers, Pulitzers and Vanderbilts once called the elaborately designed clubhouse their winter retreat—a destination reserved solely for the nation's elite.

The Club Era officially began in 1886, when wealthy members of an established hunting club decided they needed an escape from their demanding lives as captains of industry; a place they could go to relax, unwind, and decompress while surrounded by temperate weather and in relative isolation to the rest of the world. The location they decided on was Jekyll Island, and after purchasing the entire island from John DuBignon, effectively ending the DuBignon family's near-centenary ownership of the island, they quickly laid out plans for an elaborate clubhouse, with construction completed in 1888.

Over the next 60 years, the livelihood of the Jekyll Island Club could be displayed today like a typical bell curve: development exploded after the original clubhouse building was completed, with additions like The Annex and extra lodgings such as Sans Souci becoming necessary to house the growing club membership. Times were high and well-to-do families from across the nation were spending their off-seasons on the secluded barrier island through the first and second decades of the 20th century.

The Jekyll Island clubhouse was also the site of a few world-changing events in the early 1900s. A financial crisis in 1907 led bankers and government officials to find a way to centralize the nation's banking system. Key influencers decided to meet on Jekyll Island in 1910 to work on a way to restructure the nation's current banking system, thus giving birth to the Federal Reserve System, or the Fed. The year 1915 marked the first ever transcontinental phone call being placed, with the Jekyll Island Club's own Theodore Newton Vail, president of the American Telephone and Telegraph Company (AT&T), joining President Woodrow Wilson and Alexander Graham Bell on the line from one of the parlor rooms located in the Jekyll Island clubhouse.

As the years went on, club membership began to fall off, with World War I and the Great Depression having a negative impact on the lavish island lifestyle. Although the club limped along through the 1930s, World War II marked the final nail in the club's coffin, with remaining members selling the island to the state of Georgia in 1947 for $675,000 (over $7 million in today's dollars), essentially turning the prestigious private island into a public domain available for everyone to enjoy.

These days the Jekyll Island Club Hotel opens its doors to visitors seeking an elegant stroll down corridors once walked only by America's 19th century aristocracy. Guests can even hold meetings in the very room where the Fed was conceived—with a reservation, of course.

The Jekyll Island Club Hotel consists of more than just the original clubhouse. There are five separate lodgings and one church comprising today's Intracoastal resort:

————

The Clubhouse

The original building is known for its prominent turret with accompanying wrap-around verandas, immaculate interior woodwork and chimneys throughout, and fine dining via the Grand Dining Room. The Victorian setting makes this location perfect for a couple's getaway, honeymoon or anniversary.

If you're booking a room at The Clubhouse, you'll have two options: island side or river. Book the river. Rooms with a view are facing west and overlooking the Intracoastal Waterway, capping off each evening with a phenomenal sunset.

The majority of the Clubhouse rooms are comparable to name-brand counterparts and are offered at competitive rates, with discounts regularly available online by searching coupon codes for Jekyll Island Club Hotel. But if you're looking for a particularly luxurious experience–and you have the coin to back up your aspirations–you may consider booking a night in the Club Hotel's Presidential Suite.

This immaculate two-room suite sits atop the highest point of the Jekyll Island Club Hotel, and is the epitome of a world-class experience true to its Victorian derivation. Wood-burning fireplaces in both the living room and bedroom make this suite worthy of consideration during the winter months when rates tend to be lower (currently first of December through mid-March).

The highlight of a stay in the Presidential Suite is undoubtedly the spiral staircase located within The Clubhouse turret. This route leads occupants to the top of the turret where they can get a 360-degree view of the island from the crow's nest more than 40' off the ground. Considering the airport is a mere 11 feet above sea level, this 19th century turret provides quite the coastal view to a lucky few, and even comes stocked with your very own telescope for the extent of your stay.

From high ceilings and fine dining to the riverside pool and front-yard croquet, The Clubhouse is by far the most fascinating property belonging to The Jekyll Island Club Hotel.

The Annex

The Annex is the prominent addition to The Clubhouse, sitting southeast of the original building. Constructed as extra lodging for island guests in the early 20th century, The Annex offers many of the same rooms and rates as The Clubhouse. Some rooms are available with porch access facing the river, which are preferable to those facing the island side.

Staying at this historic hotel is no different than any other, although we recommend calling the front desk to book a reservation as opposed to going through a third-party booking website—you're more likely to get a better rate by cutting out the middle man and obtaining your reservation directly through the hotel.

———

Sans Souci

When The Clubhouse was packed with America's powerful and select few, the most privileged residents of the island required privacy away from the hustle and bustle of the island's social hub. Thus, Sans Souci was born.

It's impossible for anyone growing up in the U.S. to go without recognizing some of Sans Souci's well-to-do guests during the late 19th and early 20th century. According to the Jekyll Island Museum, J.P. Morgan of J.P Morgan and Company, William P. Anderson of American Cotton Oil

Company, and William Rockefeller of Standard Oil Company all had rooms located in Sans Souci.

Sans Souci is French for carefree, a term sure to define your stay in this late 19th century edifice. River-facing guest rooms with balconies, easy access to main clubhouse amenities, and skylights filling interior space with old-world ambiance make staying at this location an authentic experience for anyone seeking true-to-era accommodations.

Crane Cottage

If you've finally put a ring on that special someone's finger (or someone's put a ring on yours), and you're searching for a picturesque coastal wedding venue, then search no more.

Crane Cottage sits directly to the north of The Clubhouse, and represents a period where Jekyll's affluent property owners would accept nothing less than impeccable architectural design, flawless grounds, and exclusive accommodations (currently 13 rooms, to be exact). According to JekyllClub.com, this luxurious winter home constructed in 1917 is the most expensive seasonal cottage ever built on Jekyll Island.

The outer grounds surrounding the property are tirelessly tended and cared for, while the inner courtyard area is immaculately presented to patrons choosing to dine outdoors in an Italian-villa atmosphere.

The grounds to the south of Crane Cottage are perfect for outdoor events—especially weddings—while the meeting rooms indoors give businesses and organizations plenty of space to hold conferences and events year-round.

Cherokee

Named for the Cherokee rose gardens once surrounding the property, Cherokee is the Jekyll Club's little-known northern abode. If you're looking for a quiet, intimate experience on Jekyll, Cherokee Cottage will place you a safe distance away from the busy shops and restaurants of the central historic district. With just 10 guest rooms, a sunlit main hall, and private grounds nestled 150 yards north of The Clubhouse, Cherokee is perfect for visitors seeking an all-inclusive package of privacy, luxury, and relative solitude.

Faith Chapel: A Jekyll Island Club Sanctuary
(912) 635-4403 *(Call to ask about rentals, weddings, and events.)*

One final property you're bound to notice while strolling through the historic district is the red-shingled house of worship called Faith Chapel. The Gothic-inspired church was constructed on commission by the Jekyll Island Club in 1904, and was designated an interdenominational chapel welcoming club members of many faiths and convictions.

A few architectural points at Faith Chapel are striking, including the red-shingle siding, a one-of-a-kind Tiffany stained-glass window (which necessitates interior views to be truly appreciated), and several gargoyles hanging from exterior eaves in all directions. While many visitors may assume the gargoyles were added to ward away evil spirits, the popular architectural characters were actually designed to direct damaging rainwaters away from the side and base of buildings.

Beginning February 1st 2016, admission to Faith Chapel during tour hours will cost $5. If you already have a museum tour ticket, that ticket will automatically waive the $5 fee. According to the Jekyll Island Authority, Faith Chapel will still open its doors free of charge for organized religious services. The fee is designed to cover the rising cost of preservation to Faith Chapel, as well as tripling interior viewing hours while providing an on-staff guide to walk visitors through the chapel's robust history.

Hours of Operation

Previously open daily for unguided tours from 2 p.m. to 4 p.m., Faith Chapel's new hours for 2016 are as follows:

Monday through Saturday from 8 a.m. to 10 a.m. is free for prayer and reflection. Then from 10 a.m. to 4 p.m. the $5 fee includes a guided tour of Faith Chapel.

Sunday admission is free from 9 a.m. to 12 p.m. for prayer and reflection.

———

Jekyll Island Museum
100 Stable Road, Jekyll Island, Georgia 31527

(912) 635-4036
www.jekyllisland.com

Acting as overseers of the Jekyll Island Historic District and the many cottages and enduring properties located within its perimeters, the Jekyll Island Museum is a good first stop for anyone looking to kick-start a tour of the island's historic center. Several tour itineraries are offered through the museum, where patrons can hop on a horse-drawn carriage, tram, or go it by foot on a self-guided tour armed with only a smartphone and an e-guide rental (available through the museum) to lead the way.

There isn't too much to interact with inside the museum itself, so if you're looking for a place to kill a few hours indoors, then you should probably consider another location such as the Georgia Sea Turtle Center just a couple hundred yards north of the museum on Stable Road.

While the Jekyll Museum isn't a huge museum in the traditional sense of the word, there are several informative displays, along with a brief ten-minute movie, available inside the building worth checking out that give visitors a glimpse into Jekyll's past. One interesting story featured is that of the 19th century slave ship called The Wanderer.

According to the Jekyll Island Museum, this ship was originally designed for speed, and was to be used in oceanic competitions such as offshore boat racing. Instead, an underground slave trader out of South Carolina (importing slaves to the U.S. had been made illegal by 1858) decided to rig the vessel for a risky run across the Atlantic to pick up some 490 slaves and bring them back to Jekyll's shores to be sold. Only 400 slaves survived the journey across the Atlantic, making them the last known Africans smuggled into the United States before being sold into slavery. In a rather ironic twist of fate, the ship eventually landed in the hands of the Union Army after the Civil War commenced before finding its final resting place a decade later off the coast of Cuba in 1871.

A gift shop, restrooms, and plenty of information lie within the walls of the converted stables now being allocated as Jekyll's go-to museum. Tours vary by season, so call ahead of your anticipated arrival date to learn more. Make sure you ask about tours that take visitors inside some of Jekyll's oldest homes, too. If you have the chance to step through the doors of well-kept Victorian lodges like Indian Mound and Moss Cottage, by all means, take it.

Hours of Operation

The museum is open daily from 9 a.m. to 5 p.m. Free admission.

Jekyll Island Historic Wharf
Home of Captain Phillip's Dolphin Tours, 366 Riverview Drive, Jekyll Island, Georgia 31527

The Jekyll Wharf Marina is located on the west side of the historic district on the Atlantic's Intracoastal Waterway. The wharf is both a fully functioning marina, as well as the home of two restaurants occupying the far side of the boardwalk: Latitude 31 and the Rah Bar. Both restaurants are technically one in the same, with the Rah Bar catering to the lunch and 5 o'clock crowd on the outside, while Latitude 31 offers a more sophisticated dining experience located indoors.

The Dock Office Gift Shop is located at the end of the pier, right next to the outdoor seating of the Rah Bar. The gift shop is modest, but there's some pretty cool stuff on the inside, from beach-themed home décor to Jekyll-themed koozies for your six-pack of choice. The gift shop also doubles as a small office where you can book dolphin tours and scenic boat rides courtesy of Captain Phillip's Charters and Tours. You can give them a call at (912) 635-3152.

The Jekyll Island Club Wharf is a great location to view the setting sun towards the west across the Intracoastal Waterway, just behind a foreground of marshes and water, right from the end of the pier. It's not uncommon to see photographers and travelers pacing the boardwalk around dusk, trying to catch various perspectives of a perfect sunset across the coastal landscape of Jekyll Sound. It's also hard to go wrong with a bar right there on the dock, ready to top off your glass with your favorite beverage.

—————

Historic District Homes and Cottages

If Internet tycoons like Bill Gates, Mark Zuckerberg and Jeff Bezos had built their empires one-hundred years ago, they may have purchased their winter homes on Jekyll Island. The cottages scattered across Jekyll's historic district fill the landscape with centuries-old architecture in varying styles that speak to a time when design was tasteful and money was no object.

You may notice during the tour of homes that many of the cottages were bought and sold amongst America's elite multiple times throughout the late 19th and early 20th century. These aristocrats traded homes like 60s kids traded baseball cards, turning real-estate transactions on Jekyll Island into a real-life game of Monopoly.

One of the coolest things about many of Jekyll's historic homes is that they are available for rent. For a reasonable fee (considering the age of the homes you'll be occupying), several of the cottages, including Indian Mound, Mistletoe, and Moss, are available for grounds rentals as well as interior access for a few dollars more. These rentals are perfect for weddings and receptions, special corporate events, photo shoots, or an unforgettable "Roaring Twenties" party.

For more details and current rental rates visit jekyllisland.com.

Indian Mound

While we're not sure where the Rockefellers are spending their winters these days, around a hundred years ago it was a no-brainer: at Indian Mound Cottage, nestled on a little-known island off the coast of Georgia.

Jekyll Island was the wintertime retreat for William Rockefeller and company, and Indian Mound was their home away from home. Indian Mound Cottage remains a symbol of American opulence enjoyed by the wealthiest oil tycoons, bankers and businessmen during the early 1900s. The three-story cottage, originally built in 1892 for Gordon McKay, was purchased by William Rockefeller of Standard Oil notoriety in 1905.

William Rockefeller, brother to John D. Rockefeller, was one of the founding members of the Jekyll Island Club: an exclusive group of the wealthiest individuals in the United States at the time, with aristocratic ranks including U.S. Steel's J.P. Morgan, railroad mogul William Vanderbilt, and newspaper publisher Joseph Pulitzer, among many others. The Jekyll Island Club Hotel, the former clubhouse of the Jekyll Island elite, is now a popular resort located just 500 feet from Indian Mound's front door.

Today the property is much as it was in its original state. The Jekyll Island Museum has done an outstanding job maintaining the historic home, having recently undergone an extensive restoration of the cottage, ensuring the property remains unsullied for future generations to enjoy. According to the Jekyll Island Foundation, a twenty-three month, $280,000 restoration brought Indian Mound back to life, both inside and out. Extensive care has been taken to preserve every aspect of the structure's original form and appearance, a testament to the Jekyll Island Museum's efforts to maintain the original allure of Indian Mound.

Tours of Indian Mound, as well as other properties in the historical district maintained by the Jekyll Island Museum, are available on a daily basis. For more information on tour times contact the Jekyll Island Museum at (912) 635-4036.

Mistletoe

Directly south of Indian Mound lies Mistletoe Cottage. Construction of this home completed in 1900, making mistletoe the architectural symbol of a new century on Jekyll Island. Mistletoe Cottage was constructed in Dutch Colonial Style, identified by its large gambrel roof, flaring eave overhangs and barn-like appearance. A broad front porch facing west was no doubt conceived to ensure guests would get the most out of every coastal sunset.

If you happen to check out Mistletoe around the holidays, the cottage doesn't disappoint. You may notice a large wreath covering the French doors at the front of the home, along with several smaller wreaths decorating the western-facing stretch. It was a popular tradition among many members of the Jekyll Island Club to make their way to the island ahead of Christmas so the holidays could be celebrated in their getaway homes off the Georgia coast. A handful of fireplaces, along with the prominent chimneystacks at the peak of cottages like Mistletoe, meant keeping warm through the winter months would never be a problem for Jekyll's affluent guests.

————

Goodyear

Goodyear Cottage is an excellent representation of what Mediterranean-Style construction can bring to a southern coastal setting. One look at the elaborate eaves, rectangular floor plan, and stucco exterior should be enough to impress any architectural aficionado with an appreciation for fine construction circa 1906.

Goodyear was built by Frank Goodyear, a railroad man and lumber-business magnate from Buffalo, New York. Unfortunately, Goodyear died in 1907, just one year after construction on his Jekyll Island home was completed.

If taking in the Mediterranean architecture isn't doing it for you on the outside, then maybe the art on display at the Goodyear Shop will. The Goodyear Cottage is currently home to the Jekyll Island Arts Association (JIAA), with several displays and showcases to enjoy inside, as well as events and classes held throughout the year. Such events include pastels, pottery, basket weaving, drawing, watercolors, sculpting and more.

You can contact the JIAA by visiting Goodyear during normal hours Monday through Friday from noon to 4 p.m., Saturdays and Sundays from 10 a.m. to 4 p.m. The Goodyear gift shop is closed on holidays. (912) 635-3920.

————

Moss Cottage

If you're heading north on Riverview Drive into the historic district just past the Stable Road fork (where the asphalt ends), Moss Cottage will be the first historic home you'll see a little over 200 yards up on your right. It's easy to see where Moss Cottage derived its name from; Spanish moss fills the trees surrounding the 19th century home, providing ample shade as well as a touching coastal backdrop.

Shingle siding wraps this carefully crafted home's exterior walls, while intricate trim and traditional hardwood floors add to the cottage's southern charm. Originally built in 1896 for William Struthers, a marble-works tycoon from Philadelphia, the home was eventually purchased by George Macy, president of Carter, Macy & Company, in 1912.

———

Hollybourne

If your first impression of Hollybourne is a haunting one, you may not be too far off. According to local legends, Hollybourne is Jekyll Island's primary haunted home. With a foreboding front entranceway and grey tabby exterior casting melancholy and shadows on those touring the grounds, it definitely looks the part.

Hollybourne is one of few homes in the historic district owned by a single family, the Maurice family. Established in 1890, the home was built by Charles Maurice to accommodate his wife and many children during the island's busy season between December and March of each year. Over the years the family spent many wonderful seasons together, until the state of Georgia purchased the island from the Jekyll Island Club in 1947, effectively barring two of the remaining Maurice sisters from residing at their childhood home.

Apparently, this did not sit well with the Maurice sisters, and they went to their graves detesting the State for not allowing them to live out the rest of their days at Hollybourne. According to legend, after the Maurice sisters passed, they made their way back to their beloved Hollybourne to continue wreaking havoc with state workers; busting windows, knocking over construction materials, and leaving mysterious footprints on the property, thus delaying a multitude of renovations and improvements to Hollybourne. Of course, that could all just be the wind.

DuBignon Cottage

The DuBignon Cottage in Jekyll's historic district is unique because it gives visitors a rare glimpse into life on the island before the Jekyll Island Club landed on the scene. Prior to the sale of the island to the Jekyll Island Club Corporation in 1886, the DuBignon family owned and worked the property for the better part of a century.

The historic-district home bearing the DuBignon family name was originally intended as a simple farmhouse, built by John Eugene DuBignon in 1884. After John and his brother-in-law Newton Finney sold the island to the Jekyll Island Club—marketing it as a subtropical hunting club for the nation's wealthiest outdoorsmen—the DuBignon Cottage was used to house overflowing guests from the Jekyll Island Club Hotel until it was moved from its previous site to the location it resides in to this day.

As a side note, the DuBignon Cottage was moved over a hundred years ago to make way for a more elaborate alternative to the Jekyll Club Hotel: Sans Souci.

———

Villa Ospo Cottage

The northernmost cottage located in the historic district is Villa Ospo, just north of Hollybourne. The property of Standard Oil Company's Walter Jennings was completed in 1927, making it one of the last additions to the historic center of the island during the club era. (Villa Marianna would be the last, constructed the following year.)

The house boasts a rather simplistic style, with its rectangular shape hearkening to other Mediterranean structures on the island like Goodyear Cottage. Villa Ospo does set itself apart, however, with its prominent arched windows and doorways, courtyard and grounds, and secluded locale away from the busy Jekyll Island Club Hotel. Walks from the historic district's center north to Villa Ospo often provide visitors with a quiet and serene stroll alongside the Jekyll River.

Villa Ospo Cottage is also available to rent for indoor and outdoor events through the Jekyll Island Museum. You can reach them at (912) 635-4403.

———

Chicota Ruins

If you're making your way north from the Jekyll Island Club Hotel toward Hollybourne or Villa Ospo, you may notice a pair of lions guarding an empty lot, save a large manmade hole up a few steps and a few paces behind them. This is the site of the Chicota Cottage ruins, where the winter home of Jay Gould once stood.

Not every property was salvageable by the time the state purchased the property in 1947, and Chicota Cottage was too far-gone to repair. After family tragedy prompted the Gould family to abandon the property, the house eventually fell into ruin. Now all that remains are a hole in the ground and a pair of lion statues, still standing watch over a past marred by misfortune, and casting a steadfast reminder that even in the Gilded Age of plenty, nothing lasts forever.

———

Furness Cottage

Furness Cottage has held several titles over the last century. What began as a family home built by architect Frank Furness in 1890 soon sold to Joseph Pulitzer just six years later. After several changes of ownership, the home was turned into the island infirmary before finally settling on a bookstore with doors open to the public to this day.

For more information on the old Furness Cottage, see the section on Jekyll Books.

———

Villa Marianna Cottage

Villa Marianna is an excellent representation of authentic Spanish/Mediterranean-revival-style architecture on Jekyll Island. Clean stucco running from underneath the eaves of a tiled roof down to the exterior walls surrounding the small courtyard make the former winter home of Frank Gould look like an edifice out of the Godfather's hometown of Corleone, Sicily–minus the mafia.

Villa Marianna was constructed in 1928, making it the last club-era home to be built before World War II and the subsequent sale of the island to the state of Georgia.

John Cagle

ACKNOWLEDGEMENTS

The creation of this guide would have been impossible without the tremendous help coming from Jekyll Island's loquacious residents, workers, and guides, as well as the resources provided by the Jekyll Island Authority, which continues to do amazing work maintaining the fragile balance between human development and conservation on this diverse barrier island.

I would also like to extend my thanks to the following businesses and organizations for putting up with countless inquiries and phone calls from me for the last year and a half. Your input has not been overlooked; many thanks for taking the time to speak with me:

Segway Fun Tours
Jekyll Market
Wee Pub
Georgia Department of Natural Resources
The Jekyll Island Museum
The Jekyll Island Club Hotel

Jekyll Island Information Center
Just by Hand
Georgia Sea Turtle Center
Beachview Club Resort Hotel
Holiday Inn Resort Jekyll Island
The Westin Jekyll Island
Villas by the Sea Resort and Conference Center
Jekyll Island Campground
Three Oaks Farms
Jekyll Island Golf Club
Jekyll Island Fishing Center
Jekyll Island Mini Golf
Southeast Adventure Outfitters
Kennedy Outfitters
Summer Waves Waterpark
Jekyll Island Tennis Center
Latitude 31
Driftwood Bistro
Jekyll Beverage Center

Finally, I would like to thank my biggest supporter during this 18-month-long endeavor: my wife Megan. Without her unwavering confidence in me, I would have given up a long time ago. Thanks for believing in me, sweetie.

REFERENCES

Andrews, Kimberly M. "Species Inventory On Jekyll Island." *Applied Wildlife Conservation Lab*, n.d. Web. January 23rd 2016. <http://wildlifelab.wix.com/jekyllresearch#!wildlife-inventories/cs2n>

Associated Press. "Pests Swarm Georgia Coast." *The Augusta Chronicle*, April 22, 1998. Web. July 9th, 2014. <http://chronicle.augusta.com/stories/1998/04/22/met_226554.shtml#.VrKx2YThiV4>

Bagwell, Tyler E. "The Jekyll Island Club." *Jekyll Island History,* n.d. Web. January 3rd 2016. <http://www.jekyllislandhistory.com/jekyllclub.shtml>

Brown, Judy. "Dora—An Unwanted and Angry Visitor Arrives." *Elegant Island Living*, October 1st 2015. Web. January 4th 2016. <http://www.elegantislandliving.net/ssi-archives/dora%3A-an-unwanted-and-angry-visitor-arrives/>

Business Wire. "Westin Hotels Makes Debut on Jekyll Island, Georgia's Acclaimed Barrier Reef Island." *Starwood Hotels and Resorts Worldwide, Inc.* April 22nd, 2015. Web. August 15th 2015. <http://finance.yahoo.com/news/westin-hotels-makes-debut-jekyll-134300780.html>

Cox, Dale. "The Historic Jekyll Club." *Exploresouthernhistory.com*, 2011. Web. <http://www.exploresouthernhistory.com/jekyllislandclub.html>

"Club History." *Jekyll Island Club Hotel*, 2016. Web. January 23rd 2016. <http://www.jekyllclub.com/about-us/club-history/>

"Fishing Regulations." *Georgia Wildlife Resources Division, n.d. Web.* January 24th 2015. <http://www.georgiawildlife.com/fishing/regulations>

Franco, Michael. "Motorized Beach Umbrella Drills Itself into The Sand." n.p., December 10th 2014. Web. April 11th 2015. <http://www.cnet.com/news/battery-operated-beach-umbrella-drills-itself-into-the-sand/>

"Going to Jekyll Island? FAA Information Effective 10 December 2015."

n.p., n.d. Web. January 8th 2016. <http://www.airnav.com/airport/09J>

"Great Dunes at Jekyll Island." *Georgia Department of Economic Development*, 2016. Web. January 25th, 2016. <http://www.exploregeorgia.org/listing/2034-great-dunes-at-jekyll-island>

Hall, Michael. "Georgia Coast Still a Hotspot for Bald Eagles." *The Brunswick News*, April 29th 2015. Print.

"Hotel History." *Jekyll Island Club Hotel*, 2016. Web. January 23rd, 2015. <http://www.jekyllclub.com/about-us/hotel-history/>

" Information About Sea Turtles: General Behavior." *The Sea Turtle Conservancy*, n.d. Web. December 12th 2015. <http://www.conserveturtles.org/seaturtleinformation.php?page=behavior>

Jackson, Edwin L. "James Oglethorpe (1696-1985)." *University of Georgia Press*, December 2nd 2003. Web. January 11th 2016. <http://www.georgiaencyclopedia.org/articles/history-archaeology/james-oglethorpe-1696-1785>

"Jekyll Island." Golden Isles CVB, n.d. Web. May 11th 2015. <http://www.goldenisles.com/jekyll-island>

"Jekyll Island Master Plan 2014." *The Jekyll Island Authority*, 2014. Web. January 25th 2016. <http://issuu.com/jekyllisland/docs/8.5x11jekyll-island-final24jan2014?e=6212058/6707038>

"Jekyll Island Shopping." *The Jekyll Island Authority*, n.d. Web. January 10th 2016. <http://www.jekyllisland.com/shopping/>

Keber, Martha L. "DuBignon Family." *University of Georgia Press*, February 10th 2003. Web. January 12th 2016. <http://www.georgiaencyclopedia.org/articles/history-archaeology/dubignon-family>

Khan, Amir. "Choosing The Best Bugspray to Bug Off Bugs." *U.S. News and World Report*, June 27, 2014. Web. July 9th, 2014. <http://health.usnews.com/health-news/health-wellness/articles/2014/06/27/how-to-choose-the-best-bug-spray>

McCash, June Hall. *The Jekyll Island Cottage Colony*. University of Georgia Press, 1998. Print.

"Project Wild Teacher Resource Guide: Barrier Islands." *Georgia Department of Natural Resources*, n.d. Web. December 29th 2015. <http://www.georgiawildlife.com/node/1060>

"Rules, Regulations, Guidelines On Jekyll Island." Jekyll Island Citizens Association, n.d. Web. October 10th, 2015.
http://www.jekyllcitizens.org/jekyllinfo/rulesregs.html

INDEX

4

A

B

C

Clubhouse, 46, 174-178, 180
Courtyard at Crane, 56-57
Crane Cottage, 57, 178-179
Crane Road Trail, *See* North End Trails

D

Dairy Queen, 43-44, 80
Days Inn & Suites Oceanside Hotel, 34
Desserts, 62
Dining, 33, 41, 56-59
Doc's Snack Shop, 46-47
Dock Office Gift Shop, 122, 183
Dolphin Tour, 145
Dolphin Tours with Captain Phillip, 122
Dolphins, 145
Driftwood Beach, 155-157
Driftwood Bistro, 50-51, 118
DuBignon Cemetery, 166
DuBignon Cottage, 190-191

F

Faith Chapel, 180-181
Fishing, 97-106, 162
Fishing Charters, 105
Fishing License, 98-100
Fishing Pier, 104
Flash Foods, 19, 80-81, 111, 117
Furness Cottage, 77, 192-193
Fuse Frozen Yogurt, 63

G

Georgia Sea Turtle Center, 73-74, 127, 172-173, 182
Gift Shops, 65
Glory Beach, 157-158
Golf, 90-94
Goodyear, 74, 77, 187-188, 191
Grand Dining Room, 33, 41, 57-58, 175
Grandfather Tree Loop Trail, *See* South End Trails
Great Dunes Beach, 154-155
Gypsea Glass, 75

H

I

J

K

L

T

V

W

ABOUT THE AUTHOR

John Cagle is a freelance writer and Internet consultant living on the Florida coast. When he's not busy working with his wonderful clients, you can find him traversing America's beautiful southeastern corridor, discovering interesting places to write about from Charleston to the Florida Keys.

Be sure to visit www.coastalatlantictravel.com for the latest news, events, and stories taking place along the South's Atlantic coast.

Made in the USA
Columbia, SC
21 February 2024

32110389R00113